Cambodian Dance

Celebration of the Gods

Cambodian Dance
Celebration of the Gods

Denise Heywood

RIVER
BOOKS

This book is dedicated to the dancers
who survived the Pol Pot regime.

Frontispiece: Dancers, Angkor Wat. Bettmann Archive.

Right: *Apsaras,* Angkor Wat.

First edition published in Thailand in 2008 by
River Books Co., Ltd.
396 Maharaj Road, Tatien, Bangkok 10200
Tel: 66 2 6221900, 2254963, 2246686
Fax: 66 2 2253861
E-mail: riverps@ksc.th.com
www.riverbooksbk.com

ISBN: 978-974-9863-40-4

Editor: Narisa Chakrabongse
Design: Narisa Chakrabongse and Suparat Sudcharoen
Production Supervision: Paisarn Piammattawat

Printed and bound in Thailand by Bangkok Printing.

CONTENTS

FOREWORD
By Her Royal Highness Norodom Buppha Devi

Dance in Cambodia dates back more than a thousand years. Since the great Khmer empire at Angkor, classical ballet has always been an intrinsic part of the royal court and sacred rituals. But its fortunes have fluctuated with Cambodia's turbulent history and at times it has been threatened with extinction. Yet it has never completely died. Its spirit has lived on in new generations of dancers eager to revive an art form that is the essence of our cultural identity and the living expression of our ancient heritage.

Now, at last, Cambodia is at peace. But while the country is developing, the status of dance is still fragile. It faces an uncertain future. When it was inscribed on the UNESCO list in 2003 as a "Masterpiece of the oral and intangible heritage of humanity", it was a milestone in the history of dance and a tribute to the devotion and sacrifices made by all the members of the Royal Ballet. Like the temples of Angkor, it is to be preserved for the world. But it is still limited by our country's economic conditions and maintaining a troupe of more than fifty dancers is expensive.

Thus, the success has been gradual. As a dancer since childhood, I have been completely committed to helping rebuild the ballet. Support has come from my father, the former king Norodom Sihanouk, who has always been a patron of the arts, and from our present king, His Majesty King Norodom Sihamoni, a dancer and choreographer, so that dance continues to be one of the jewels of Khmer culture, despite the setbacks of history.

Today, the Royal Ballet operates under the aegis of the Royal Government of Cambodia, and dancers study at the Royal University of Fine Arts with ballet masters who have been granted a status that ensures their security. The troupe perform at traditional ceremonies and ancestral rituals and welcome important guests. Through the support of friends and colleagues outside Cambodia they have toured internationally on three continents.

As a result, experts on the dance of Southeast Asia have praised the dedicated work of dancers, ballet masters and civil servants in bringing this tradition back to its former glory. But much more still needs to be done. I hope that as the recognition of Cambodian dance increases, this will bring much needed international help. The perpetuation of our classical dance is not only for Cambodia but for the whole of humanity.

Therefore, every effort to make Cambodian dance known to the world is invaluable. My thanks to Denise Heywood, a sincere friend of Cambodia and the Cambodian people, whose research and photographs celebrate the dance. Her book is both a reference to the history of this ancient art form and a contribution to its future.

Opposite: **Princess Buppha Devi dancing for Jackie Kennedy, 1967, by kind permission of Philip Jones Griffiths.**

INTRODUCTION

Dancing *apsara* from the Bayon, 13th century. (PP)

Seda and Rama, Phnom Penh, July 1928, Musée Albert Kahn.

"The role of all artists in the world is to teach people to love good rather than evil. We are peace messengers. We dance to ask the gods to help our country. People are born and die. But the country never dies." Proeung Chhieng, choreographer and dancer, survivor of the Pol Pot regime.

In September 1993, while I was living in Cambodia, I was staying in a small wooden guest house on stilts down an unpaved side street in Siem Reap, which was just a village then. It was run by a gentle and charming man, Ty Sopath, and his wife, both survivors of the Pol Pot regime. He spoke French, which he had had to conceal from the Khmer Rouge for fear of being killed. He called up to me one afternoon, and I went out on to the wooden verandah.

"Madame Denise," he said, looking up at me eagerly, "there is a performance of classical dance by local children at sunset at Angkor Wat. Would you like to come? I think you would enjoy it."

Of course I would! He told me to meet him on the road to Angkor in an hour as he would be driving all the dancers in a van used for tour groups. Like most Cambodians, he had about three different jobs, working in a government office, organising tours, running a guesthouse and now, it appeared, helping dancers with their performance.

I arrived at the meeting point just as the van with *Bopha Angkor Tourism* on the side was pulling up. As there were hardly any tourists in the country then, it had been commandeered for the occasion. I got in and we drove off. It was filled with dancers, many of them tiny girls, barely six years old. They sparkled in scarlet and emerald goldspun costumes covered with sequins, ornate golden tiaras, jewels, bangles and earrings. Their little faces with rounded cheeks and upturned noses were finely powdered, and they had black kohl around their huge brown eyes, glitter under their eyebrows and gleaming red lipstick, with their shining black hair swept up into intricate golden headdresses, revealing delicate little necks. Fragrant pale yellow frangipani flowers were fastened over each ear. Their tiny hands had red painted fingernails, and one of

them held a silver chalice filled with more frangipani petals. They looked like exotic dolls. Serious and poised, they stared at me but did not dare to smile or talk. Their perfect behaviour was part of the rigorous training needed to become a ballet dancer.

When we arrived behind the eastern entrance to the temple and parked, they all got out in a line and walked in a procession past the northern galleries of carved *bas-reliefs* and around to the west front of Angkor Wat which faces the long sandstone causeway. The traditional *phleng pin peat* orchestra of xylophones, oboes, drums and gongs was already in place, with nine musicians, several of them old men, survivors of the killing fields, who had passed on their skills to younger pupils. They had set up the inevitable loudspeaker and I braced myself for the amplified sound of evocative Khmer music which dates back 2,000 years.

As the sun started its descent, casting a golden glow over the temple, the dancers began performing scenes from the *Reamker*. The children danced with such gravity, remembering every step they had been taught, their little hands bending backwards in the traditional movement of the *apsaras*, their small bare feet gliding across the stone. The gestures were very slow, stylised, with the knees bent. A boy playing Hanuman, leader of the monkey army, entered in a glowing white and silver costume with a mask, doing slow motion cartwheels. The performance ended as the sun set, an orange orb slipping behind the trees, suffusing the sandstone with hues of gold and copper, and the dancers tossed the frangipani petals from the silver bowls to the audience.

The sight of those children dancing seemed to resonate with a sense of new order in Cambodia. As they danced in rhythm, I reflected on the symbolism of Angkor Wat, a temple built to reflect divine harmony. The dancers' performance seemed like a return to creativity after a period of destruction, the cosmic after the chaotic.

On the way back, I sat next to Heng Dara, an elderly baker from the cavernous kitchens below the old, dilapidated Grand Hotel. Another survivor from the Pol Pot regime, he told me in French that his wife had been a dancer at the Chanchaya Pavilion in Phnom Penh. He knew all the dances off by heart and started telling me the stories.

"At the end they perform the Flower Blessing Dance, *Robam Chuon Po*. The final gesture is called *Bai Pka*, Tossing The Flowers. It brings good luck. I am so happy to see the dance revived after the long years of war. I thought I would never see it again."

His eyes were alight with enthusiasm, animating a face prematurely aged by the suffering of starvation and forced labour.

"*C'est la joie, Madame*," he said. "It is a joy."

Royal dancer as Sovann Maccha, 1910, Pierre Dieulefils.

Dancer at the Royal University of Fine Arts, Phnom Penh.

Khmer dancer by Auguste Rodin. Musée Rodin, Paris.

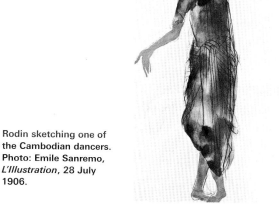

Rodin sketching one of the Cambodian dancers. Photo: Emile Sanremo, *L'Illustration*, 28 July 1906.

Detail from freize of dancers, Angkor Wat, 12th century. (PP)

"It would seem that dancing came into being at the beginning of all things, and was brought to light together with Eros, that ancient one, for we see this primeval dancing clearly set forth in the choral dance of the constellations, and in the planets and fixed stars, their interweaving and interchange and orderly harmony."
Lucian, Assyrian-Roman Scholar, from *The Dance of Shiva*, Ananda K Coomaraswamy

Dance is transcendent. As primal, rhythmic energy, it surpasses the human and expresses the soul. It is universal, evolving in a unique way in every society, in a multiplicity of forms, from sacred ritual to tribal war dance.

In Cambodia, classical dance is the quintessence of the country's identity. An art form that is religious in origin, its traditions hark back more than a thousand years to the great Khmer empire which flourished from the 9th-15th centuries AD. Dancers performed in temples and were the living embodiment of *apsaras*, celestial dancers carved on the walls of Angkor Wat. Their role was so revered that the king created the Royal Ballet to act as intermediaries between the monarch and the spiritual realm. They lived within the palace and many were princesses. With their sacred symbolism, graceful gestures and exquisite costumes, they came to represent the soul of Khmer culture.

But in the 20th century, this spiritual and artistic heritage was almost destroyed during the genocidal Pol Pot regime. 90 percent of the dancers were murdered. A few escaped the killing fields. Barefoot and starving, they walked back to Phnom Penh. Today, they have taught a new generation of dancers. This heralds not only the revival of the spirit of a nation devastated by war but the rebirth of ancient traditions.

Dance and drama have been fundamental to societies throughout history. They reflect not only the myths of a culture, but religious and political views, highlighting events that relate to the worldview of the audience, rendering the drama even more poignant. They "hold as 'twere the mirror up to nature," as Hamlet's memorable phrase expressed.

Reflecting reality, the re-enactment of a range of intense emotions affects the audience which, in ancient Greek dramatic theory, is moved by the representation, *mimesis*, and purged *catharsis*. *Mimesis* originally meant the imitation of a person or a god through dance or gesture, according to Aristotle (384-322BC). Artists, the philosopher claimed[1], imitated permanent rather than transient modes of thought and therefore embodied the belief system of a culture. Aristotle's theories on the role of dramatic art and its ability to transport an audience mirror the Hindu theory of *Rasa*. In Sanskrit *rasa*, which means the 'sap of plants', describes the aesthetic pleasure derived from works of art and, at a higher level, signifies the transcendent pleasure and bliss that unites artist and viewer, as if flowing from one to the other, as they share a heightened rapport. The audience is an essential part of the sacred performance.

These theories are especially relevant in Cambodia where dance-drama, much of it drawn from the Hindu epic the *Ramayana*, came to be seen as the most important artistic activity at the court and, by extension, throughout the countryside in less sophisticated forms such as folk dances and shadow puppetry. While it entertained, its religious dimension was paramount: it was always a ritual offering, a connotation that faded from Western drama. Dance-dramas offered a completeness and a harmony that was missing in mundane reality. They reflected the myths and structure of society and provided a spiritual framework for dilemmas which cannot be resolved in everyday life. While good eventually triumphs over evil, the forces of vice and virtue in the epics are perpetually in balance. Major characters are never destroyed because good and evil must survive in order to define each other.

This counter-balance is central to dramatic representation and reflects early Greek theories relating to Dionysos, god of drama. His natural, primitive energy is contrasted with Apollo who represents order, visual beauty and self-knowledge. The combination of these opposing elements was necessary for the production

of tragedy, and the Hindu epics, especially the *Ramayana*, articulate classical dramatic function perfectly.

The alternating allegiances and moral dilemmas echo not only the Apollonian and Dionysiac aspects of drama, but also Hindu theories of the duality of existence, with its eternal balance of opposites. The one cannot exist without the other. They could also be construed as metaphors for Cambodia's history. In a country dominated by the biggest religious monument in the world, a place of mystical beauty, one of the most evil social experiments was conducted. As the violence was unleashed, it was as if that balance was inherently unstable.

In a society where almost everything was destroyed, reviving these rituals and myths helps to redress the balance and restore the soul of a nation. By re-enacting their myths societies can repeat what their gods, ancestors and heroes did in the beginning. The magic of this repetition makes the theatre what it had been at the time of its Dionysian origins, a place of holy communion with life itself. Re-enactment leads to resolution and spiritual harmony and social cohesion follow. Dance and drama not only reinstate the past but lay the foundations for the future.

The reward for the work of the dancers and all those connected with them came in 2003 when the Royal Ballet of Cambodia was inscribed by UNESCO as a Masterpiece of Oral and Intangible Heritage. Like the historic temples of Angkor which are a UNESCO World Heritage Site, Khmer classical dance has been classified as part of the heritage of humanity.

This book looks at the origins of Cambodian dance and its role in the history of the civilisation of Angkor, examining its religious foundations and symbolism. It charts the development during the French colonial period when it was politicised, a function of the court rather than the temple, and its popular image in the 20th century, before the devastation of war. It touches on the horror and tragedy of the Pol Pot regime, when culture was destroyed, recording some of the surviving dancers' stories. It shows the work of those survivors and how their dedication has resulted in the revival of dance, music and shadow puppetry, bringing back into existence a living art that is a reflection of the spiritual foundation upon which Cambodian culture is based. It concludes by questioning the role of dance and its religious nature in the future.

Prince Norodom Sihamoni, now King of Cambodia, photographed in 1995 by Franck Nolot.

[1] *Poetics*, Aristotle.

CHAPTER 1 ANGKOR AND DANCE

Opposite: **Dancers Angkor Wat.**

"If we are indifferent to the art of dancing, we have failed to understand not merely the supreme manifestation of phsyical life, but also the supreme symbol of spiritual life." Havelock Ellis, *The Dance of Life.*

A female dancer in shimmering silk and glittering gold emerges like a vision with extraordinary slowness and grace from a niche within a carved stone temple wall. She is a luminous apparition, a sculpted divinity coming to life. The sumptuous whiteness of her costume, enriched by the gold of her head-dress towering above her black hair, radiates an aura of magic that is enhanced by her exquisite, ethereal movements.

With her hands joined in prayer, she raises them to her forehead then her lips, then lowers them as they separate and move through small arcs, turning her wrists and bending her long slim fingers backwards in circular gestures of such delicacy that they resemble

Angkor Wat.

wings. Her face is serene and impassive, with its finely chiseled features enhanced by such elaborate makeup that it seems almost a mask. Knees bent and back arched, she keeps her bare feet, sparkling with jewelled anklets, firmly on the ground, gliding imperceptibly back and forth with infinite slowness, while she communicates through the language of myriad subtle hand movements, emulating the stone friezes of antiquity.

But this is more than just a performance. In Cambodia, classical dance is a celebration of the gods, a sacred ritual to please the ancestral spirits. In Khmer mythology, the gods themselves were cosmic dancers and every performance was regarded as an offering to them. In an art form whose origins are divine, the performers are a link between the earthly and the heavenly realm.

Dance evolved with the construction of Hindu temples. Between the 9th-15th centuries AD, the Khmer kings at Angkor expressed their religious beliefs through the prolific building of majestic stone temples, culminating in Angkor Wat, built between 1113-1150, the biggest, most brilliantly designed religious edifice in the world. Dance was so integral to these beliefs that it was represented on the temple walls in the form of carved *apsaras*, celestial dancers. Dancers, in turn, performed in the temples and were the living embodiment of the images on the walls. The temple was a recreation of the Hindu cosmos, and the dancers symbolised its rhythms.

The dancers' role was so important that the kings created their own royal ballet, the *lakhon luong.* Their performances would have been auspicious, a way of communicating with the ancestors in the heavenly realm. Although the exact nature of their dances is not recorded, they probably formed part of the rites at funerals, coronations and important events, as well as in ceremonies to promote rain.

At Cambodian New Year, in April, the hottest period before the rainy season, the dancers re-enacted sacred legends intended as offerings to propitiate the

12

Apsara, **Central Sanctuary Angkor Wat**.

spirits responsible for rainfall. The lunar and monsoonal cycles dictated life for the Khmers, with the tropical wet and dry seasons governing harvests, and the prosperity of the kingdom depended on water and its distribution throughout the growing seasons. But as the monsoon rains might come too early or too late, prayers were offered up. The king would conduct a *buong suong* ceremony to invoke the help of the *tevoda*, the celestial spirits, when the country faced droughts or floods. It was believed that divine spirits would possess the dancers. If their dances were received favourably, the deities would bestow their blessings on the country and the prayers of the king would be granted. The correct performance of these rituals was important for the kings who believed themselves to be *devarajas*, god-kings, and it reaffirmed the connection between heaven and earth that was intrinsic to Cambodian religion and culture.

Religious Symbolism

Since ancient times, dance and architecture have been regarded as the two most important sacred arts. Both are concerned with the use of space and rhythm. In classical Greece, dance was regarded as an activity of the gods and performed in temples as a holy ritual. In Cambodia, these two essential arts were inspired by Hinduism. Through maritime trade with the Indian subcontinent, the Khmers came into contact with that country's religious, artistic, architectural and aesthetic ideas which influenced and enriched their own. As in India, temple worship became central to the Khmers' religious practices and with it, dance. Sacred dance, recorded in historic Sanskrit texts such as the *Rig Veda*, ancient hymns forming part of four books of sacred knowledge composed between 1500-1200 BC, were performed in Indian temples as offerings to the deities.

In Hinduism, the relationship of dance and architecture is especially significant. Temples were built in accordance with *Vaastu shastra*, the science of Indian architecture founded on divine geometry, transforming the mystical numerical basis of the universe into static form, while sacred dance used space to recreate the rhythms of the cosmos. The temple was a recreation of the Hindu cosmos on earth, built to maintain the harmony of the celestial and terrestrial spheres. Like the temple, dance is sacred in form and in content.

The Hindu sculptor, according to Titus Burckhardt[2] must know the rules of the ritual dance as it is the first of the figurative arts, since it works with man himself. "Sculpture is thus attached to two radically different arts," he writes. "Through the technique of the craft it is related to architecture, which is essentially static and transforms time into space, whereas the dance transforms space into time, by absorbing it into the continuity of the rhythm." These two poles of Hindu art, sculpture and dance, engendered what Burckhardt described as the most perfect fruit of Hindu art: the image of Shiva dancing.

Shiva as *Nataraja*, the Lord of the Dance, is one of the most widespread images in Indian art and was absorbed into Khmer iconography, although with less frequency. In Hinduism, a complex, polytheistic system of rites and ceremonies, the creative force of the universe is the god Brahma. After Brahma has brought the cosmos into existence, it is sustained by the god Vishnu and destroyed by the god Shiva, only to be recreated once more by Brahma. This trinity of gods, constituting destroyer, creator and preserver, form the triad of the *Trimurti* that became incorporated into the Khmers' beliefs.

Shiva's cosmic dance, ushering the world into existence at the beginning of a creative cycle and destroying it at the end, reinforces the fundamental principle of dance as divine activity. The Hindu perception of time is cyclical, not linear and creation is thus a continuous process. With the image of a god as dancer, dance itself is an offering to the gods and a continuation of cosmic rhythms.

The dance of Shiva represents his five activities: *Shrishti*, creation, *Sthiti*, preservation, *Samhara*, destruction, *Tirobhava*, illusion and *Anugraha*, emancipation. Surrounded by a ring of flames, Shiva balances on his right leg, his foot crushing the dwarf of ignorance, while the left leg is raised in a balletic attitude to signify ultimate release. His many arms in circular motion symbolise his numerous personalities, and his hands hold his divine attributes, such as a drum to beat out the rhythm of creation and a ball of fire to represent destruction. This dynamic image of pure energy is at the same time a vision of transcendental calm.

Of this cosmic dance, art historian Ananda K Coomaraswamy[3] writes: "No doubt the root idea

14

An Indian representation of Shiva Nataraja, Lord of the Dance.

Left: **Shiva Nataraja from Banteay Samré. (PP)**

Buddhist Monk meditating at Angkor Wat.

the natural forces of earth and water and to be a conduit with the spiritual realm which controlled the harmony of their union. Cravath writes: "Whether the two great forces were expressed as female and male, earth and water, or dark and light, their interplay was conceived as a contest or battle expressible in dance, which was the embodiment of their rhythms …"

As a symbol of the universal rhythm, dance evolved gradually from the hallowed precinct of the temples to that of the royal court and in Cambodia, as in India, became a royal ritual, reaching the heights of artistic refinement. It was so highly valued that dance became even richer in symbolism and texture. But its spiritual dimension in no way diminished. If anything, it deepened. The relationship of the dancer to the audience had – and still has – profound significance. Through the dancers' performance, the audience transcends the ordinary, mundane world and enters the realm of the gods, an experience that is heightened by the elaborate costumes, music and ritualised movements.

Dance, therefore, was an integral part of religious and royal life at Angkor, where all art was sacred. These artistic traditions continued even after Theravada Buddhism was absorbed into the kingdom. Like Hinduism, Buddhism arrived peacefully, through

behind all of these dances is more or less one and the same, the manifestation of primal rhythmic energy … A great motif in religion or art, any great symbol, becomes all things to all men; age after age it yields to men such treasure as they find in their own hearts. Whatever the origins of Shiva's dance, it became in time the clearest image of the *activity* of God which any art or religion can boast of." Thus Shiva's dance is divine action, creating the rhythm of existence.

This rhythm of dance is central to the thesis of Paul Cravath[4], who believes that the female dancers provided a mystical regeneration of the fertility of the land. In addition, the architecture of Angkor embodied spiritual values that were fundamental to political unity and symbolised irrigation systems that harnessed the waters of a river that changed direction twice a year to create the kingdom's prosperity. Angkor is a *mandala*, a cosmic diagram ritually traced on the ground prior to the building of the temple, a diagrammatic symbol for a field of energy and a generative symbol in architectural form. Its intention is to reveal

Buddhist Monk praying at Angkor Wat.

Dancing *apsaras* on lotus flowers, from the Hall of Dancers, Preah Khan.

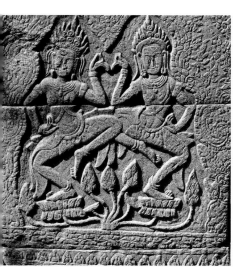

trade, when the religion, inaugurated by the Buddha, Prince Siddharta Gautama in the 6th century BC, spread across Southeast Asia from India in the succeeding centuries. A philosophy in which there is no god – Buddha in Sanskrit means 'enlightened one' – it was the dominant creed at Angkor in the late 12th century, followed by periods in which Buddhism and Hinduism alternated. In Cambodia religion is syncretic, a blend of Hinduism and Buddhism, ancestral worship and animism. Buddhist temples such as the Bayon incorporated Hindu and Buddhist imagery, while Hindu ceremonies, including dance, remained part of Khmer traditions.

Early Dances

How these dances began, and through what external influences, is not recorded. Early indigenous dance forms in Cambodia, connected with animistic worship in the region, may have blended with Hinduistic traditions from India from which sacred dances evolved. These were possibly influenced by the ancient treatise on Sanskrit dramaturgy, the *Natya Sastra of Bharata*, dating from about 200AD, thought to have been written by the sage Bharata, with origins in Brahma's fifth *Veda*. In this manual for theatrical performance, the gestures of the hands had a supreme role in conveying meanings, and were categorised according to the movements of a single hand, both hands and dance hands, whereby the *mudras* of palms, fingers and arms constituted a special art form. No such text has been discovered so far in Cambodia, but other influences may have blended with these forms as the Khmer empire stretched across Southeast Asia. As the ritual aspects of dance were so integral to Khmer culture, the movements which expressed them must have evolved among the Khmers themselves.

Whatever its early origins, the perpetuation of dance relied on oral transmission and if it was not practised, it disappeared. To preserve the sacred dances, importance was placed on perfecting gestures handed down from master to pupil since they were rarely recorded in any form of texts. By repetition their spiritual value increased and ensured that inherited

The Hall of Dancers, Bayon.

forms were preserved. This is a contrast to Western, secular ballet, which developed in the court entertainments of Renaissance Italy and France, where the impulse was to find new ideas and forms.

In Cambodia, each dance is an act of worship to the *krus*, the gurus or teachers of the dance, who have near-deity status. This echoes the *guru-shishya parampara*, the Indian tradition of teachers and disciples, that dates back to the times of the *Vedas*. So revered are the teachers, possessors of knowledge about centuries' old traditions which is passed to their pupils, that special prayers are accorded to them and gifts are brought to honour them. Before each performance in Cambodia, dancers enact a *sampeah kru*, a ceremony in which they seek permission to dance, asking their gurus to make this the best performance possible. Every Thursday, singled out as 'teacher's day', a special ceremony is enacted to thank their teachers in an ancient prayer ritual, the *buong suong*. Respect for the teacher ensured that each acolyte adhered to the principles that would otherwise be lost, and each pupil in turn taught their skills to a future dancer, ensuring the continuation of knowledge.

Yet in spite of these revered practises, dance must have changed and evolved over the centuries. Historically there is little evidence of what dance actually looked like. The *bas-reliefs* of *apsaras* at Angkor Wat, although referred to as celestial dancers, are, for the most part, depicted in static poses rather than in motion, and it is their hand gestures, the *mudras*, which allude to dancerly poses. Just as Indian temples incorporated a *nata mandap*, a hall of dancers, so do Jayavarman VII's temples such as Preah Khan and the Bayon. In such representations, the dancers who are almost naked, have both legs oscillating outwards, knees bent, balancing on one leg with the other raised, in the *ardhaparyanka* pose, a step that no longer exists within the restrained, stylised female dances of today, but resembles more a posture of male dance. The movements radiate energy and ecstasy, and looking at them one can almost hear the rhythm of drumbeats. In contrast to the demure *apsaras* of Angkor Wat, such female dancer motifs at the Bayon appear at all entrances, possibly suggesting a cult to Hevajra, a multi-armed Tantric dancing deity, a version of Heruka, attendant of Shiva, and a symbol of enlightenment.[4]

In addition to the dances suggested in these images, individual dancers must have brought their own artistic and spiritual temperament to their craft over the years, even though their own creativity was suppressed in training themselves to memorise the examples of their teachers, forcing their bodies to obey a fixed formula. While they were vehicles rather than creators of a complex inheritance of expression, there must have been some element of extemporisation, enriching the interpretation while maintaining a reverence for tradition.

Dance Today

Today there are about 20 theatrical forms. They range from classical dance and theatre, a legacy of the court, to circus and folk art, incorporating ceremonial and ritual dances, performed throughout the country at weddings, funerals and new year festivities. There is pure dance, *robam*, ancient classical dance, *robam boran*, and dance-drama, *lakhon*. The classical dance, *lakhon kbach boran*, has a repertoire of about 60 dance pieces, including the sacred *apsara* dance, *robam*

Buddhist monk, Angkor Wat.

Hall of Dancers, Preah Khan.

Dancing *apsara* with *pin peat* orchestra.

Opposite above left: **Burmese dancer as Ravana from the *Ramayana*, painted by Sir Gerald Festus Kelly (1879-1972) © Christies Images, 2008.**

Opposite above right: **Two Siamese dancers from collection of Dennis George Crow.**

Opposite below: **Balinese dancers performing the *Ramayana*, Ubud, Bali.**

apsara, and 40 *roeung*, dance-dramas. Accompanied by the musicians of a *pin peat* orchestra, the drama is mimed by the actresses, while the text is sung by a female chorus offstage. In addition, there is *lakhon kaol*, male masked dance-drama, where the story is chanted, *lakhon poul srei*, female masked drama, *lakhon sbaek thom*, shadow theatre, many folkloric and musical forms such as *lakhon mohori* and *lakhon yike*, story telling such as the *chapei*, accompanied by a lute, and an improvised folk chant, the *lakhon ayai*. While inspired by ancient myths, these latter also draw on contemporary events and can have a political or satirical edge.

The *Ramayana* and the *Mahabharata*, performed in dance-dramas, puppetry and shadow play, appear throughout the Southeast Asian region from Laos and Thailand to Bali, Burma and Java, appearing in Cambodia in the 16th or 17th century, with the *Ramayana* reinterpreted as the *Reamker*. Khmer dance is often compared to its Thai counterpart, with which

there has been considerable artistic interaction, as well as that of Laos. Resemblances with the sumptuous dances of Bali and Java, where the epics are played, also exist, most especially in the elaborate hand gestures. Like Khmer dance, Balinese hand movements have less to do with the progress of the plot and more to do with embellishing expressions of the body, with some similar movements of the torso to Khmer dance. The sense that dancers, always grounded and invariably on flexed knees, are close to the earth is also a part of the Balinese tradition. But the Khmers lack the extraordinary eye movements of Balinese dancers.

But just as the temples of Angkor show that the Khmers absorbed an enormous number of external artistic ideas, particularly those of India, so innumerable external factors must have shaped the dance which then evolved into the pure Khmer ballet as it is interpreted today.

Angkor and dance **19**

Maps of Cambodia and Angkor.

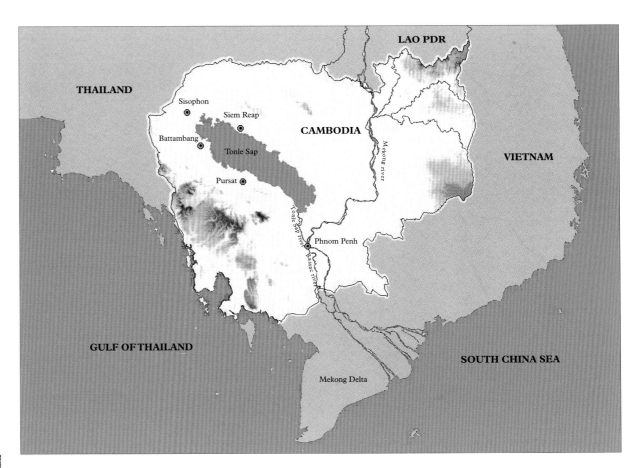

Shiva Nataraja, Angkor Wat.

What is remarkable, however, is that dance has endured in any form at all, given the repeated rupture of tradition throughout the centuries. Cambodian dance has become almost extinct several times, particulary in the 20th century, and yet survived; its history is intertwined with the history of Cambodia itself.

Cambodian History

Cambodia's past is steeped in legends. The earliest relate that the country originated with the marriage of a *nagi*, a dragon princess, with a foreigner. Another version describes a Brahmin called Kaundinya who married a *naga* princess named Soma after shooting an arrow into her boat. He later constructed a capital in a country name Kambuja, a name of northern Indian origin and linked with Kambu Svayambhuva, an Indian prince, married to Mera, an *apsara*, from whom

the first Khmer kings descended, making the mother of all Khmers a celestial dancer. This legend appears in inscriptions dating from 947 AD.

Archaeological evidence reveals numerous small independent states in the region then referred to as Funan and Chenla by Chinese traders, whose religious ideas developed through contact with maritime trade with India. Court musicians from Funan travelled as part of a diplomatic mission to perform for the emperor of China as early as 243 AD. Female dancers were dedicated to the Hindu temples of Chenla as early as the 6th century. No written documents have been found so information comes from epigraphy. There are 1,200 carved inscriptions in stone at Angkor, the earlier ones in Sanskrit, under Indian influence, and the later in Khmer, translated by the 19th century French scholar George Coedès. The earliest inscription in Khmer is 611 AD. The inscriptions are real works of art and imply that Khmer scholars

Suryavarman II bas relief.

Wives of Suryavarman II.

towards the rising sun, which is auspicious. Angkor Wat faces the setting sun and darkness, symbol of death, as it is believed to be a mauseoleum for the king. It is aligned with the vernal equinox. On the morning of March 21, as the sun rises up over the eastern entrance, it has a spectacular solar alignment between the west end of the western causeway and the central tower 500 metres away, rising at the exact apex of the central tower and illuminating the entire western causeway. Numerous mathematical theories about Angkor have been expressed by scholars, showing how every measurement at Angkor is determined by specific laws of proportion, since the dimensions are in harmony with the mystical numerical basis of the universe and time itself.

Angkor Wat is covered with superbly carved bas-reliefs. Those of the third gallery, in particular, are of outstanding richness, containing thousands of figures and depicting scenes from the *Mahabharata* and the *Ramayana*, as well as images of Suryavarman II himself in a historic procession, battles of *devas*, gods, and *asuras*, demons, lurid evocations of the tortures of the 32 hells of Khmer mythology, as well as the pleasures of the heavens, the myth of the Churning of the Ocean of Milk, the battle of Lanka, and many other legendary scenes. Among all these are the *apsaras*, numbering some 1,860 in all. Their presence evokes the pleasures of the heaven of Indra, king of the gods, and their proliferation reinforces their symbolic role as the rhythms of the Hindu cosmos, of which the temple is a recreation.

The 17th century Cambodian poet Pang praised what he called these ethereal inhabitants of heaven[5:]

"These millions of gracious figures filling you with such emotion that the eye is never wearied, the soul is renewed, and the heart never sated! They were never carved by the hands of men. They were created by the Gods, living, lovely, breathing women."

Apsaras

Apsaras, Sanskrit for celestial nymphs, or heavenly dancers, were associated with water in Hindu mythology, created during the churning of the Ocean of Milk, flying up from the foam. Their watery origins symbolise their association with fertility.

The Churning of the Ocean of Milk is a Hindu cosmogonic myth, a story of creation. At Angkor Wat the magnificent carving of the scene occupies the east gallery wall, symbolically facing the rising sun. One of

Vishnu above the turtle Kurma from the central section of the Churning of the
Ocean of Milk. The *apsaras* can be seen emerging from the foam at the top. (PP)

the most important scenes ever carved in stone, it is inspired by the Hindu epic, the *Bhagavata Purana*, part of the early Indian texts. It focuses on the search for *amrita*, the elixir of immortality, and is an endeavour to impose order out of chaos. In a tableau of perfect symmetry, the *devas* and the *asuras*, the gods and the demons, are involved in a tug of war with a churning pivot in the form of the serpent Vasuki, the five-headed *naga*, who is wrapped around Mount Mandara. Vishnu is at the centre of this struggle, orchestrating the action, supported by his avatar, the turtle. In Indian mythology the *apsaras* were so beautiful that neither *devas* or *asuras* would marry them and so they became *Suranganas*, wives of the gods, and *Sumad-atmajas*, daughters of pleasure, and assumed the role of heavenly dancers in Indra's Paradise.

Apsaras depicted in the Churning of the Ocean of Milk are full of movement. Some are flying, legs bent; other are shown in the *ardhaparyanka* pose, a dance movement like a *plié*. This is different to their portrayal elsewhere in the temple where most appear standing still rather than in motion. Some scholars have debated whether these latter ones should be described as *devatas*, deities, or *apsaras*. Author and artist Sappho Marchal[6] opted for the former, admitting that *devata* is a vague term. Here I will refer to them all as *apsaras*.

Within a funerary monument the *apsaras* bring not only a vivid representation of life but that of the life force itself, of youth and fecundity, females at the peak of physical perfection. The sanctity of the temple is counterbalanced by these representations of earthly pleasures.

Like the temple on which they are carved, they have perfect proportions and symmetry. The sculptors not only adhered to the classical proportions but also lavished them with endless details. Almost naked, their breasts full and seductive, they are adorned only with extravagant head-dresses and ornate jewellery, while a thin layer of transparent silken material clings to their slender hips and thighs. Their slim bodies stand straight, balanced evenly on both feet, hips square, rather innocently, instead of swaying in the provocative *tribhanga* pose with hips slanted and weight on one

leg, as they do in Indian and Cham sculpture. The perspective of the *apsaras'* feet must have perplexed the sculptors, as both are turned rather comically to one side, like a puppet's, in a position in which it would be difficult to actually stand.

Each one is slightly different, both in adornment and facial features, but they all possess a mysterious half smile, known as the Khmer Smile, alluring yet shy, immediate but other-worldly. With their faces framed by a diadem that has swept away their hair, many have features that are flawless and exquisitely proportioned, as if created in a heaven where all things are perfect. They are archetypes, original models of which everything else is a representation. They embody ideal Khmer beauty and are iconic images throughout Cambodia today. Their perfection makes the *apsaras* rather like Khmer supermodels to whose looks many women aspire.

Apsara, Angkor Wat.

Apsara in *tribhanga* pose, Cham Museum, Danang.

Apsaras, Angkor Wat.

Apsara showing her teeth.

Apsara with enigmatic smile.

Dancers copy them. The graceful movements of the *apsaras*' arms and hands are regarded as the origins of the movements of Cambodian dance which, in turn, appears so sculptural. Perhaps they were based on dance as it was practised in the 12th century. Whether this is historically accurate or whether dances have been reinvented is debated. Sasagawa Hideo[7] writes that contemporary dances 'mimicking' the bas-reliefs are a means for the audience to imagine that the dance is of the 'Angkorian' tradition. He refutes this, claiming that the so-called 'traditions' have often been invented, since the 'idealised Angkor' has been a frame of reference only since the colonial period. Nevertheless, the hand gestures, together with the serene faces, enigmatic smiles, jewellery and head-dresses of the *apsaras*, are emulated by dancers today in their search for a classical frame of reference.

The role of the *apsaras* reflects the influence of Hindu art which exalted feminine beauty not only as fertility, but as a manifestation of universal rhythm. Throughout India temples are carved with female divinities and, like dance in Hinduism, they are an expression of both religious devotion and erotic love, as Hindu sculpture transmutes sensuality by imbuing it with spiritual resonance.

While the outer structure of many Hindu temples displays the female, the feminine creative function, the centre often contains a *lingam*, the phallic symbol of Shiva. Thus the temple is a symbol of the balance of male and female, echoing the Hindu belief in the perpetual balance of opposing forces. But, whereas Indian sculptures of goddesses are more voluptuous, and even include images of erotic union, symbolic of divine union, Khmer sculptors were more subtle in their interpretations of femininity as an expression of spirituality. The *apsaras* possess a sense of virginal innocence, even though they are nearly naked.

The *apsaras* are sometimes described as purely decorative and highlight the absence of earthly women depicted at Angkor. In a kingdom whose prosperity was based partly on the existence of a slave class, women would have been chattels of men, especially among the patrician classes. The dancer's role, while exalted, was that of a concubine of the king. But symbolically their role is of fundamental importance. Paul Cravath[8] writes that in relation to the temple, the *apsaras* and, by extension, dancers, are a representation of the two

natural forces or principles in confrontation, the Feminine and the Masculine. "In the Angkorean period we see the elaboration of a tantric symbology of the archetypal Feminine-Masculine contest and union in architecture, in the bas-reliefs, in public celebrations and in dance." Thousands of dancers served in the temples as offerings to the ancestral spirits who could influence the cosmic interaction, particularly, of earth and water.

The fundamental action of the Churning of the Ocean of Milk, he writes, is the union of the king with the waters, activated by the two forces. "The conflict is not merely between *deva* and *asura* in the Indian sense, but rather represents duality in general … moon and sun, Feminine and Masculine." The serpent is the spirit of the water and the churning resulted not only in the elixir of immortality but also in the creation of the *apsaras* who flew up from the foam. Thus, with the serpent, they represent the balance of the duality of the universe. The role of the many dancers at Angkor was to embody what the *apsaras* represented on the spiritual plane.

Nothing at Angkor was created solely for decoration. Everything was charged with spiritual significance and this religious ardour infuses the sculptures with transcendent qualities. Even the stylistic detail of placing the *apsaras* singly, in pairs, trios or in lines, adds to the rhythm of the sculptural composition.

Some of the most alluring and richly embellished *apsaras*, holding lotus buds, are to be found close to the central sanctuary. Were the exquisite faces based on real women? Were they the features of queens or courtesans within the royal court? While at other temples the faces are generic, at Angkor Wat there are different personalities. Some have enchanting, humorous details, such as one who is showing her teeth, unique among the *apsaras*. Another sticks out her tongue, and yet another, whose arm is around her companion, extends her fingers teasingly to touch her companion's breast. Studying the *apsaras* around the temple, one finds some that were started and never finished, and it is evident that the first section of the *apsara* to be carved was her breasts.

The head-dresses, which must have been based on real ones made of gold, are composed of floral and vegetal motifs. Sappho Marchal, daughter of Henri Marchal, drew the *apsaras* in detail in 1927[9]. She showed how the flower shapes are predominantly

Apsara touching her companion's breast.

Apsara sticking out her tongue.

Pair of *apsaras* whose breasts shine from the touch of many hands.

Unfinished *apsaras*.

Right: **Pair of *apsaras* showing feet pointing to one side.**

Two *apsaras* with intricate head-dresses.

Apsara with elaborate coiffure.

Pair of *apsaras* photographed by John Thomson.

Hip belt on *sampot* with intricate lotus flowers.

those of the lotus, the sacred flower of Hinduism. It is a recurring symbol throughout the temples of Angkor, notably in the quincunx of towers at Angkor Wat which are in the form of upturned lotus buds. The towers of the Bayon, with the face of the Buddha, are topped with lotuses. The *apsaras* are surrounded with images of the flower, depicted in profile, or flattened against the head-dress, *mkot*. The head-dresses have spires like the towers of Angkor Wat and are decorated with flattened lotus buds. Each *apsara* holds a lotus bud, sometimes provocatively, and their jewellery abounds with lotus motifs, especially the multi-layered necklaces and dangling ear-rings. Other flowers include those of the coconut palm and areca palm. Even some of the hip belts of the *sampots* are sculpted in sumptuous detail, showing hanging jewels in the form of lotus flowers.

Not everyone was enamored of the *apsaras*' ubiquitous presence, however. The devoted Catholic Paul Claudel, brother of the sculptor Camille Claudel, visited Angkor with George Groslier in 1912, during the French protectorate, and described with horror "those *apsaras* with their Ethiopian smiles, dancing a kind of sinister cancan on the ruins." Angkor, he said, "is one of the most accursed, the most evil, places that I know."[10]

But other early visitors succumbed to their charms, such as the Scots photographer John Thomson who took the first photographs of the *apsaras*, and indeed of Angkor (see Chapter 2), in 1866. These vital early images are still used today for reference by archaeologists and conservationists, such as the German Apsara Conservation Project, whose work has succeeded in preserving those *apsaras* that had become damaged by time and weather. Thomson's black and white photographs of the *apsaras* are especially evocative and enthralled the Royal Geographical Society in London, where they were first shown, giving the West its first glimpse of the religious art of the Khmers.

Carved Bas-Reliefs

Even scenes depicting battles, such as the magnificent panel of the Battle of Kurukshetra from the *Bhagavad Gita*, the most important section of the *Mahabharata*, symbolically facing west and the setting sun, seem more like ballets than battles. The ranks of soldiers are so finely chiselled, their legs bent in movement, and arms raised in graceful poses, that they flow in harmo-

Above and below: **Battle of Kurukshetra, Angkor Wat.**

Above and below: **Battle of Kurukshetra, Angkor Wat. (PP)**

Face tower, Bayon.

Bayon temple.

Dancing Hevajra, late 12th century,
30 cm. (PP)

nious groups and formations across the panels. Lit by the evening sun as it touches the stone, they appear to turn gold. Throughout the temples, images ranging from fighting soldiers to monkey gods are shown in acrobatic postures that echo dance movements.

Jayavarman VII

After Suryavarman II, the last significant king was Jayavarman VII who ruled between 1181-1220 and built the huge, mystical temple of the Bayon, a structure to rival Angkor Wat. Jayavarman VII was a devout Buddhist and under his influence, Buddhism took root in Angkor. The face towers of the Bayon, thought originally to number 54, are conjectured to be the image of the Buddha, but may also be the king's portrait, fused with that of the Buddha[11]. The most important sculpture of the king, one of the finest Khmer sculp-

tures in existence and now in the National Museum in Phnom Penh, shows him deep in meditation. He built not only an impressive city, Angkor Thom, but more temples than any of his predecessors, as well as hospitals. At the same time the kingdom expanded under his influence and he fought numerous wars, including one against the Chams.

Among the icons from this period is a bronze Hevajra, the tantric dancing deity, a deification of the ritual invocation to the *vajra*, or thunderbolt, in the Bayon style from Banteay Kdei temple. This dynamic Mahayana Buddhist divinity, now in the National Museum in Phnom Penh, radiates the energy of dance, with eight heads and 16 hands in graceful, sweeping poses that capture the sense of movement as the figure balances on two corpses on a lotus flower. It reinforces the powerful affinity of dance with ritual.

At this time, Jayavarman VII donated thousands of dancers to the temples of Preah Khan and Ta Prohm,

Detail from the Hall of Dancers, Ta Prohm. (PP)

Hall of Dancers, Ta Prohm. (PP)

as ritual offerings, which suggests that the religious role of the dancers remained the same as that under Hinduism. The temple of Ta Prohm, dedicated to Jayavarman VII's mother, has Sanskrit inscriptions relating to the 615 dancers who, along with 18 high priests, 2,740 officials and 2,202 assistants, helped to maintain the temple. Preah Khan, the temple of the 'sacred sword', dedicated in 1191 to his father, as much a university as a monastery, housing masters and students, contains among its many sanctuaries a 'hall of dancers.' The lintels here are carved with bas-reliefs of dancing *apsaras*, in the *ardhaparyanka* pose, animated images that pulsate with energy.

[1] Titus Burckhardt, *Sacred Art East and West*, Perennial Books, 1967.

[2] Ananda K Coomaraswamy, *The Dance of Shiva*, Noonday Press, 1957.

[3] Paul Cravath, *Earth in Flower: The Divine Mystery of Cambodian Dance Drama*, Dat Asia Inc, 2008.

[4] Peter E Sharrock, *Bayon: New Perspectives*, River Books, 2007.

[5] Pang translated by Etienne Aymonier, *Textes Khmer*, 1878.

[6] Sappho Marchal, *Khmer Costumes and Ornaments of the Devatas of Angkor Wat*, 1927.

[7] Sasagawa Hideo, *Post Colonial Discourses on the Cambodian Court Dance*, 2005.

[8] Paul Cravath, *Earth in Flower: The Divine Mystery of Cambodian Dance Drama*, Dat Asia Inc, 2008.

[9] Sappho Marchal: *Khmer Costumes and Ornaments of the Devatas of Angkor Wat*, 1927.

[10] Paul Claudel, *Journal*, October 1921.

[11] *Bayon: New Perspectives*, River Books, 2007.

"Dance has always been ritually associated with temple and monarch in Cambodia …. In few societies can it said that dance is so greatly respected as a rite of self per petuation." Paul Cravath, *Earth in Flower.*

Even though dance was so integral to the court of the Khmer kings, it featured only slightly in a description[1] of the kingdom in 1296 by a Chinese emissary, Chou Ta Kuan. Written as Angkor's power had started to decline, following the end of Jayavarman VII's reign, it revealed the author's enchantment with a country "where clothes are not necessary, where rice is easy to buy, women easily persuaded, houses easy to furnish and business easy to manage." His mention of dance is limited to a note that: "The eight is the month of *ai-lan* (*ram*) or dancing. Every day actors and musicians are summoned to the royal palace to perform the *ai-lan.*"

Otherwise, he refers only to the enormous number of palace girls and concubines. When the king leaves his palace, he observes, "300 to 500 palace maidens, gaily dressed, with flowers in their hair and tapers in their hands, are massed together in a separate column. Close behind come the royal wives and concubines, in palanquins and chariots. …. From all this it is plain to see that these people, though barbarians, know what is due to a Prince." He also mentioned that when a beautiful girl is born, "no time is lost in sending her to the palace." Doubt has been sensibly cast on the veracity of this report, suggesting it may have been construed largely from hearsay. This seems all the more likely when considering the emissary's fantastical descriptions of the sexual appetites of Khmer women whom, he claims, are eager to have relations with their husbands immediately after childbirth or else they go in search of alternative partners. Perhaps this was more wishful thinking than established fact. However, his description confirms the existence of the royal harem, a tradition that continued into the 20th century.

Engraving of Angkor Wat after Louis Delaporte from F. Garnier's *Voyage d'Exploration en Indochine*, 1873.

as 1930, border territory was still disputed, as in the case of the Khmer temple of Preah Vihear, on the border of Thailand, which was given back to Cambodia after Prince Sihanouk went to the international court at The Hague.

The status of Cambodian dance was improved by the interest of the French after Cambodia became a protectorate and the French preserved the court traditions of which the dance was an integral part. King Norodom, having been brought up in the royal palace in Bangkok, maintained a court of luxury and pomp, not dissimilar to that of Siam. The king and his wives, as well as the princesses, princes and courtiers, wore exquisitely woven silk and brocade outfits with embroidered slippers and coiffed hair, often pulled up into jewelled headpieces, with ornate earrings. They wore glittering rings on their fingers and a profusion of bangles and bracelets around the ankles and wrists. The king's dancers, since the sartorial embellishments of Ang Duong, were equally extravagantly attired in brocade and silk with golden head-dresses and abundant jewellery. The court was a small, rarefied world in contrast to the rest of the country which was an entirely rural, peasant population and the exotically costumed dancers, with their short cropped hair and faces made up with white cosmetics, looked utterly different from the Cambodian peasants dressed in cotton, their skin burned dark brown from the relentless tropical sun.

The dance troupe of King Norodom included numerous Siamese dancers who had returned with him from his stay in Bangkok, so much of the nomenclature of Khmer dance was Siamese. The classical Cambodian court forms of female dance drama, *lakhon kbach boran*, shadow play *nang sbaek* and mask dance *lakhon kaol* are comparable to Thailand's *lakhon fai nai*, *nang yai* and *khon* respectively, but the influence of Siam in Cambodia weakened as that of France's increased. Two disparate cultures were about to converge.

The fragility of the living arts, most especially dance, was recognised by French scholars who, highly sensitive to their aesthetic qualities, set about studying and resuscitating them. But Cambodian culture was also politicised in the colonial period and the sacred art became incorporated into a newly defined Cambodian nationalism.

Young prince at the Royal Court,
Fonds Iconographiques des Missions Étrangères de Paris.

Above and right: **Princess and a prince at the royal court, Fonds Iconographiques des Missions Étrangères de Paris.**

Below: **Princess at the royal court, Fonds Iconographiques des Missions Étrangères de Paris.**

Above and right: **Dancers at the Royal Court, Fonds Iconographiques des Missions Étrangères de Paris.**

Dancers performing in the Chanchaya Pavilion, Phnom
Penh, 1921. Collection Léon Bussy, Musée Albert Kahn.

[1]Chou Ta Kuan, *Report on the Customs of Cambodia*, 1296.

[2]Charles Emile Bouillevaux, *Voyages dans l'Indochine 1848-
1856*, 1858.

[3]Henri Mouhot, *Travels in Indo-China, Cambodia and Laos*,
1863.

CHAPTER 3 EARLY FRENCH PROTECTORATE

The Royal palace, Phnom Penh.
Photo: Pierre Dieulefils.

"The characters of Cambodian theatre belong to a world of legend and fantasy …" Danses cambodgiennes, Samdach Chaufea Thiounn, the first Cambodian writer on dance.

From 1863 Cambodia came under French hegemony and in 1887 became part of the Union of Indochina, incorporating Vietnam, with Laos added in 1893. During Governor-General Paul Doumer's tenure (1897-1902), French rule was homogenised and bureaucratic procedures unified. A beguiling capital was created in Phnom Penh with elegant colonial buildings on wide tree-lined boulevards and it soon became known as the Paris of Asia. Between 1889-1897 Huyn de Verneville, the French administrator, built bridges, canals and docks and embellished the city with 360 grand houses. The central police station, railway station, library and post office were among the many attractive buildings, painted traditional yellow like the palace. King Norodom had started construction of a new royal

palace in 1873, auspiciously facing east, with a throne room and a Silver Pagoda with a floor of solid silver tiles. Added to this during the French era, in 1913, was an open sided performance hall for the royal ballet dancers, the Chanchaya (meaning moonlight) Pavilion, or Royal Tribune, with its elegant spire, still used today. It was based on an identical plan to an earlier, wooden building, constructed by King Norodom. Dances are performed in a space marked out in the centre of the floor, with guests seated around it. Singers stand at the northern part of the space, while musicians are placed at the southern end. Costumes and jewellery were placed in rooms beneath the throne room.

This period of architectural and artistic growth brought a revival of dance fostered by French scholarship and literature on the subject. French interest in dance stemmed from their own considerable traditions which dated back to Louis XIV, the Sun King (1638-1715). A patron of the arts, he organised performances at the court in which he himself danced, appearing as

The Napoleon III Pavilion within the grounds of the Royal Palace, a gift from France, 1876.

The Chanchaya Pavilion within the grounds of the Royal Palace was built specifically for dance performances.

French building in neo-classical style,
Phnom Penh.

Hotel Le Royal, built in 1929.

Right: La Bibliothèque, the French-built
library, 1926.

Colonial villa, now the offices of UNESCO.

Ornate French colonial villa.

King Norodom by John Thomson.

Apollo, the sun god, as his extravagant reign reached new heights in a ceremonious way of life for the privileged aristocracy.

He opened the first Académie Royale de Danse in 1661, the first public theatres were constructed, and Molière, whose troupe performed for the king from 1665, wrote 15 *comédies-ballets*, mixtures of plays with dance interludes. Since then, Western dance terminology has been in French, although the word 'ballet' derives from *ballare*, the Latin verb to dance – hence a ball – and from the Italian *balletti*, a figured dance, reflecting the simultaneous rise in Italy of dance and opera. In some ways the Sun King, with his solar symbolism, could be compared with Suryavarman II, as Louis, like the Khmer monarch, regarded himself as a god. Louis' love of dance took root and even after the turmoil of the French revolution, dance was maintained and developed into one of France's richest performing traditions.

French interest in Cambodian dance, a form which was almost exclusively female until the 20th century, was tainted by the fact that King Norodom, who continued to live in luxury even though his royal power had diminished, maintained troupes of dancers who were, in effect, part of the royal harem. This was composed of hundreds of women. Although an age-old

practice, one that had exerted a strange, prurient fascination for the Orient over many Occidentals, was nevertheless morally repugnant to the monogamous French who considered it a barbaric form of slavery and tried to reduce its numbers. (Yet, at the same time, Huyn de Verneville kept a high society Cambodian concubine, Dame Ruong, but this relationship too was quickly thwarted by a disapproving Paul Doumer[1].)

However, the king's predilection for the harem, together with opium and alcohol, was recorded by numerous visitors, including John Thomson, who photographed the sovereign dressed in splendid military style regalia, but observed him almost naked while watching a dance performance, stretched out decadently, chewing betel nut and smoking. The king, who had five wives and sired scores of children, punished any women of the harem who were unfaithful, sometimes violently, implementing a draconian system of laws where infidelity was considered as treason. Inevitably the palace seethed with intrigue, although this was based on rumour as few outsiders had access to the harem. It must have been a place of intense frustration and boredom and many of the women, unless favoured by the king, took solace in, and dedicated themselves, to dance. When artists such as

Louis XIV dancing as Apollo with lyre.

George Coedès.

Angkor Wat photographed by
Pierre Dieulefils.

Henri Parmentier.

George Groslier came to write about the dancers[2], some of the descriptions were tinged with pity.

La mission civilisatrice

In spite of this political discord, the colonisers avoided the brutal and exploitative forms of empire, bringing instead what they called a *mission civilisatrice*, a civilising mission, borne of their belief that it was a duty to bring prosperity, Christianity and the benefits of civilisation to non-Western countries. The idea of the mission civilisatrice, defined less magnanimously as "educating natives into 'our civilisation,' " by later critics such as Edward Said[3], was nevertheless embraced by many influential thinkers of the time. Although the aim of France was obviously profit, the French mission included education and the native adoption of the French language. It brought an appreciation of the artistic heritage of the colonised countries as well as an exchange of intellectual ideas. Learned institutions were created such as the École Française d'Extrème Orient in Hanoi in

1907, and the School of Cambodian Arts, a precursor to the Conservatory of Performing Arts and the Royal University of Fine Arts created during the 1960s. After Angkor was ceded back to Cambodia in 1907, the École Française d'Extrème Orient began clearing the site and examining the monuments.

Under the auspices of these institutions came a succession of archaeologists and art historians who studied the culture of Indochina, including dance. Notable among these were Groslier who, among many other accomplishments, wrote two books on Cambodian dance. Others included Bernard-Philippe Groslier, his son, Auguste Pavie, Roland Meyer, Henri Parmentier, George Coedès, Leon Fomberteaux, Lunet de la Jonquière, Victor Goloubew, Etienne Aymonier, Henri Marchal, his daughter Sappho Marchal, Jean Commaille, Madeleine Giteau and many more. Some dedicated their entire lives to their research. The romance of Angkor's reconstruction by French scholars was almost as evocative as its original creation by the Khmer kings.

Henri Marchal.

George Groslier.

AU CAMBODGE
La crémation solennelle des restes du roi Norodom

Cremation of King Norodom, 1904.
Bridgeman Archive.

Pierre Loti's paintings of dancers from *Un Pelerin d'Angkor*.

The restoration of Angkor and interest in dance inspired Cambodians with pride in their culture and history and were among the most valuable legacies the French left. That a Frenchman, Henri Mouhot, was attributed with the so-called discovery of the site of Angkor also increased prestige for France. Frenchmen such as August Pavie, an officer with the colonial administration who loved Cambodia and Laos, learning both languages, and writer Pierre Loti, *nom de plume* of Julien Viaud, a naval captain, were both fascinated by the dancers and mentioned them in their books. Writing in 1901, Pierre Loti evoked the magic of a performance:[4]

"It's this evening at 9 pm that old King Norodom will receive me. This governor had the great kindness to tell him that I was more than a simple *aide de camp*, but a representative of France. It seem that there will be a grand reception which will feature the *corps de ballet* of the royal court.

"One of the doors, all of a sudden, seemed heavy and mysterious, as if about to announce something supernatural. Then one of them started to open: a little adorable creature, almost like a chimera, suddenly came into the middle of the room: an *Apsara* from the time of Angkor! Impossible to have created a more perfect illusion; she has the same features because she is of the same pure race, she has the same enigmatic smile, eyelids lowered and almost closed, the same chest of a young virgin, barely covered by a silken wrap…."

These 'little adorable creatures' were among 500 dancers that Norodom kept in the palace, in three troupes. Princess Khoun Tanh was the star of the main troupe, Princess Khoun Prea Nieth the leader of the second and Princess Man Soun the third. But, in spite of memorable performances such as Loti described, their numbers diminished considerably after Norodom's death in 1904.

King Sisowath by Pierre Dieulefils.

King Sisowath and his dancers

In a shrewd political manoeuvre, the French passed over his sons and crowned Sisowath (1904-1927), his half brother and son of Ang Duong. A francophile, he was more compliant with their aims, a disposition encouraged by their supplying him with the opium to which he became addicted. During Sisowath's reign the number of dancers was reduced to only about 100 or so as he was unable to support them on the allowance accorded him by the French who were reluctant to waste financial resources on dancers.

Yet, ironically, the dancers' reputation in France had grown to such a degree that only a visit by them would satisfy the insatiable curiosity they had aroused. The dancers had become a symbol of royalty and a pawn in the Franco-Khmer political arena. So, under George Bois, who organised exhibits for the Colonial Exhibition of 1906 in France, it was decided to invite the king himself, so that he would bring his dancers, and in the May the king took half this troupe on tour to the exhibition in Marseilles. The sacred dance of Cambodia was about to become an international phenomenon.

[1]Penny Edwards *Womanising Indochina: Colonial Cambodia* in *Domesticating the Empire*, Julia Clancy-Smith and Frances Gouda, 2007.

[2]George Groslier, *Le Theatre et La Danse au Cambodge*, 1929.

[3]Edward Said, *Culture and Imperialism*, 1993.

[4]Pierre Loti, *Un pelerin d'Angkor*, 1901.

Rodin sketching at the Villa Glycines, July 1906. Photo: Émile Sanremo.

"I contemplated them in ecstasy … When they left, I was in the shadow and in the cold, I thought they had taken with them all the beauty of the world." Auguste Rodin on the Cambodian dancers.

The dancers arrived in June 1906 with King Sisowath to perform at the *Exposition Coloniale* in Marseilles, a historic visit that would bring the dancers international recognition. It was the first visit ever made by a Cambodian monarch to France which had ruled over Indochina since 1884. It was a subtle irony that France, now a republic, welcomed a king who reigned but did not rule, who then had to swear allegiance to his colonial masters and attend a colonial exhibition. Nevertheless, as King Sisowath had come to the throne only two years earlier, it was a prestigious visit. But it was his entourage of dancers that was the jewel in his crown.

The royal party had departed from Saigon on board the *Amiral de Kersaint*, on 10 May, bringing the ballet troupe of nearly 80 members, including a retinue of musicians, singers, jewellers and dressers. The king's principal dancer was his own daughter, Princess Soumphady. She was a slight, fine-boned figure but, when they disembarked, her scintillating appearance, with red betel-stained teeth and a costume sparkling with diamond brooches and medals, offset with black silk stockings and gold embroidered shoes, had an intoxicating effect on the crowd eagerly waiting on the quayside at Marseilles. One of those who witnessed the flamboyant spectacle was Roland Meyer who was inspired to write a romantic novel about a Cambodian dancer[1].

The dancers, their teeth chattering with the unaccustomed cold, were then accommodated in Marseilles. To protect them from inquisitive onlookers, they stayed in the Villa Glycines where they reportedly ate three hearty meals a day, used forks rather than chopsticks and preferred baguettes to rice.[2] Their first performance was in the festival hall of the Grand Palais in Marseilles. The king took pride of place, seated on a velvet armchair, and regally signalled his dancers to enter. Dazzling in their silk and gold outfits, radiating charm and sweetness, they immediately had the audience in raptures.

King Sisowath then embarked on official visits, leaving the dancers temporarily in Marseilles. Far from worrying that he may have abandoned his dancers to alien foreigners, he realised that he had left an incomparable example of the sophistication of his country. The visit to France had suddenly made him aware of the power and value internationally of an art form that had been the exclusive preserve of the Cambodian royal court.

Three days later the troupe danced at the Colonial Exhibition to an enthusiastic crowd, including journalists such as Lacarre who, in *Le Petit Journal*, compared them to *apsaras*. Even though they were completely covered in their heavily loaded costumes, the dance lost "nothing in the suppleness of its movements or

elegance of its line." He admired their agile feet and nimble hands. "In them fade away the last undulations of the body, whose movements are inspired by the coiling of the Naga, the serpent-god …" The dancers became a major attraction as one performance followed another and, finally, they were taken to Paris.

Performing first at the Elysée Palace on 1 July, the dancers then appeared on the open air stage at the Pré Catalan Theatre in the Bois de Boulogne on 10 July. An audience of 3,500 people attended, far more than could be seated, resulting in a huge crush. Auguste Rodin (1840-1917), the great French sculptor, was among them and was so captivated that he instantly started to draw the dancers. He was 66 years old at the time. Dance was the last major artistic theme in his work. Fascinated by the dynamic of movement throughout his life, Rodin was inspired and intoxicated by the grace of the dancers and his drawings reveal the excitement of this extraordinary encounter between the ageing sculptor and the exquisite young girls of the Cambodian royal troupe. "It is impossible to see human nature carried to such perfection," he cried. "There have only been them and the Greeks."

Programme for the Cambodian dance performance at the Pré Catalan Theatre, 5 July 1906.

Rodin sketching one of the Cambodian dancers. Photo: Émile Sanremo, 1906.

Cambodian dancers performing in the
Bois du Boulogne, 10 July 1906.

King Sisowath's dancers in the grounds
of the Royal Palace, Phnom Penh.
Photo: Pierre Dieulefils.

King Sisowath's royal dancers.
Photo: Pierre Dieulefils.

Orchestra and dancers from the Royal Palace.
Photo: Pierre Dieulefils. Before 1909. Gelatin bromide negative on glass.

Cambodian dance troupe in costumes for the *Reamker*, with Hanuman in the foreground centre. Photo: H. Badouin, 1906.

He had never seen such small dancers, with supple bodies able to bend to every demand of the ballet. This new form of expression inspired him to sketch and paint some enchanting watercolours. "I drew with infinite pleasure the little Cambodian dancers who came to Paris not long ago with their king. The tiny movements of their agile limbs were strangely and marvellously seductive," he claimed.

"The great Rodin, was ecstatic …" wrote the journalist P B Gheusi of *Le Figaro* newspaper, "over the little virgins of Phnom Penh, whose immaterial silhouettes he drew with infinite love …" In the ensuing days Rodin spent all his time drawing the dancers in the gardens of a villa in the rue Malakoff where they were staying. "The friezes of Angkor were coming to life before my very eyes," exclaimed Rodin. "I loved these Cambodian girls so much that I didn't know how to express my gratitude for the royal honour they had shown me in dancing and posing for me."

But the dancers then had to return to Marseille on 12 July to perform at the Colonial Exhibition. Rodin, in his enthusiasm, dropped everything to follow them on to the train, drawing incessantly, with the paper on his knees, and remained with them until they boarded their ship home, on 20 July. "I contemplated them in ecstasy," he cried, "when they left, I was in the shadow and in the cold, I thought they had taken with them all the beauty of the world."

Rodin drew them obsessively to capture every nuance of their subtle dance patterns, concentrating on the arms and hands, his sculptor's eye seizing on the essence of the dance. He was fired with passion for the aesthetics of their movements, so different from those of European ballet. Although the pace of classical dance resembles a series of still tableaux, Rodin's images, with their interplay of fast and slow lines flowing one into the other, give a sense of speed and energy that seemed to reflect the artist himself.

Rodin sketched prolifically throughout his career, studying the human figure and its movements before starting on his sculptures. With a pencil or a paintbrush he would capture in a few swift strokes the fleeting details of motion, endlessly studying the way it transformed the human body. Then, armed with sketches, he would start work on clay. As well as drawing 150 pictures of the Cambodian dancers, he did vivid sketches of other dancers of the period, in particular Isadora Duncan and Loie Fuller and, later on, Vaslav Nijinsky. With the Cambodian pictures he applied the same artistic techniques. A superb draftsman, he concentrated his entire attention on the figures, expressing through line, form and rhythm not only the movements, but the inner meaning and soul of the dance. His attention was less on the faces and all on the gestures. As with his nudes, he highlighted the drawings with flat watercolour tints with a slight gradation that created harmonies of rare refinement. These watery hues were especially effective when he depicted the dancers in simple silk wraps, *sampots*, as well as lavish costumes, showing the diaphanous fabrics in gentle colours, as in Le Printemps, where the pink robe resembles the gossamer wings of a butterfly. Facial features are barely shown, so that the overall impressions are of elegant, youthful figures in mid-pose, with shimmering fabrics that cling to, and move with, the limbs.

These images were enhanced when, on arriving in Marseilles on a Sunday, he went to the Villa Glycines, where the dancers were staying, only to find he had run out of paper. Unable to find an art shop open, he bought wrapping paper from a grocer's and used that. The result enriched the texture of the pictures, giving them the grey, pearly quality of antique Japanese silks. The transparent, unfinished look of Rodin's pictures seems to symbolise the ephemerality of dance, an elusive art that exists only in performance.

At a deeper level, Rodin was struck by the timeless and universal nature of the movements, which transformed this unknown art into a manifestation of the universal principle of the 'unity of nature' through time and space. "They made the antique live in me ... I am a man who has devoted all his life to the study of nature, and whose constant admiration has been for the works of antiquity. Imagine, then, my reaction to such a complete show that restored the antique by unveiling its mystery". He had been similarly inspired by seeing Chola bronzes from India and understood immediately what he called the 'divinity of human form' that he saw in them. When shown a photograph of a sculpture of the god Shiva, he praised its transcendental power. "Like something divinely ordered, there is no hint of revolt in this body: everything is in its place ... The gesture is graceful enough to compete with the Medici Venus, shielding her charms with her arm, while Shiva seems to protect himself with the ingenious gesture, " he wrote in a French journal.

What astonished him, he claimed, was to rediscover the very principles of classical art in a Far Eastern art that had been unknown to him until then. "Confronted by pieces of very ancient sculptures, so ancient that no date can be assigned to them, the mind gropes it way back towards their origins across thousands of years; and then, quite suddenly, living nature appears, and it is as though the ancient stones had come to life once more! The Cambodians gave me all that I used to admire in ancient marbles, supplementing it with the mystery ... of the Far East. How enchanting to find humanity true to itself across time and space." He told George Bois that he believed dance was 'animated architecture,' referring to the harmony of time and space.

Rodin was profoundly moved by the connection of religion and art in Cambodian dance. "When religion disappears, art disappears too," he concluded. "All Greek and Roman masterpieces, all our own master-

Hand of a Cambodian dancer, 1906. Graphite and watercolour on cream vellum paper.

Cambodian dancer, 1906. Graphite, watercolour and gouache on cream vellum paper, originally white.

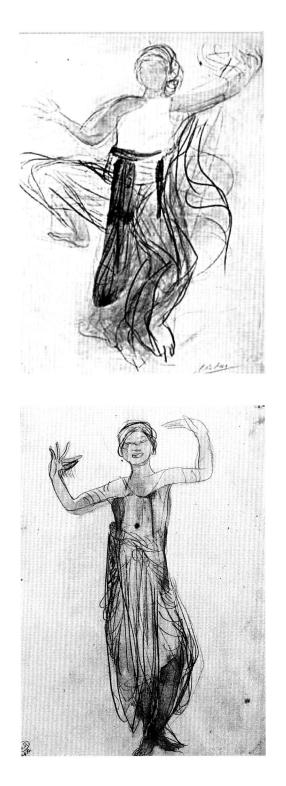

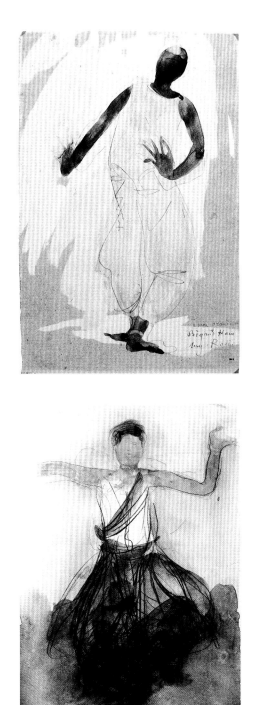

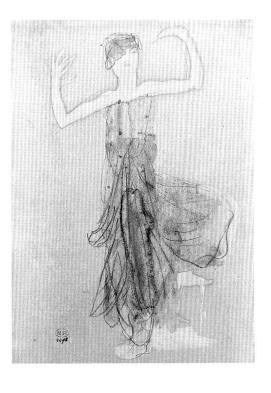

pieces, are religious. Sisowath and his daughter Soumphady … have taken great care to maintain the strictest orthodoxy in these dances, which is why they have retained their beauty. After all it was the same idea, varying only in form, which preserved art in Athens, Chartres, Cambodia – everywhere. Just as I recognise classical beauty in the dances of Cambodia, so I recognised Cambodian beauty at Chartres, shortly after my visit to Marseilles, in the posture of the great angel, which is not so very far removed from a dance movement."

Rodin's response, not only as a great sculptor but as an admirer of architecture and antiquity, showed his intellectual brilliance. He understood Cambodian dance, going beyond the visual aesthetics to the quintessence of the sacred art form. The poet Rainer Maria Rilke, who was Rodin's secretary until 1906, recognised the sculptor's perception and wrote in a letter to him in November 1907, "You have penetrated … far more than you would believe into the mystery of Cambodian dance. Your methods, through the 18th century and Greece, epitomise the eternal gestures of the Orient and evoke the holy writings of those movements of the soul that remove the weight from blessed and ingenuously docile bodies."[3]

Yet amid the divine and romantic aura, the dancers were also human and Rodin reportedly had to bribe them with gifts to make them pose. His favourites were three 14 year olds, Sap, Souna and Yem. Georges Bois, the fine arts delegate of the French colonial administration, watched him and noted that the dancers would stop posing and start pouting until Rodin went off to the *Nouvelles Galeries* department shop to buy toys for them. Then, said Rodin, "these divine children who dance for the gods hardly knew how to repay me for the happiness I had given them."

An article in the newspaper *Le Petit Marseillais* even referred to the 'darlings' who enthralled Rodin but who did occasionally put a foot wrong. On their last day, when they went to be photographed by H Baudouin, delegate of Cambodia to the Indochina Commission, Princess Soumphady, leading the troupe, stepped in some cow dung down a muddy alley in Marseilles. Mad with rage, she threw her arms in the air and flung

herself on the ground, whereupon all the adorable little dancers threw themselves into the dust, decked in their finery, and rolled unceremoniously around. "They were very sweet, the Cambodians," it concluded, "but they weren't without their shortcomings."

Not everyone was enamoured of their looks. One surprised observer[4] criticised their hard and close-cropped hair, "their figures like those of striplings, their thin, muscular legs like those of young boys, their arms and hands like those of little girls, they seem to belong to no definite sex. They have something of the child about them, something of the young warrior of antiquity and something of the woman. Their usual dress, which is half feminine and half masculine, consisting of the famous *sampot* worn in creases between their knees and their hips and of a silk shawl confining their shoulders, crossed over the bust and knotted at the loins, tends to heighten this curious impression. But, in the absence of beauty, they possess grace, a supple, captivating, royal grace, which is present in their every attitude and gesture."

The day of their departure, 20 July, found Rodin in bed, exhausted, so he never actually saw them sail away on the *Amiral Ponty*. George Bois witnessed the departure ceremony and applause at the quayside and wrote: "Like a flight of marvellous birds, lost for an instant in our grey sky, they left, the little Cambodian dancers, and they will never return!"[5]

Rodin's drawings were exhibited to great acclaim in Germany as well as France. With so much publicity, the dancers were a *success fou* in France, propelled into the international area, exciting huge interest in Cambodia. That Rodin became their champion was an unforeseen bonus for here was someone who, while dazzled by their earthly beauty, understood the religious dimension. Yet, a few decades later, this sacred art was almost extinct.

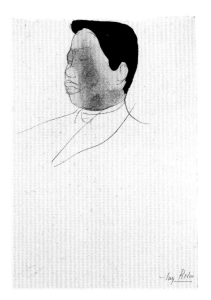

Portrait of King Sisowath, 1906. Graphite, watercolour and gouache on cream vellum paper.

[1] Roland Meyer, *Seramani, danseuse khmere*, 1922.

[2] Hughes Herpin, *Rodin and the Cambodian Dancers*, Editions du Musée Rodin, 2006.

[3] Rainer Maria Rilke to Rodin, *Rodin and the Cambodian Dancers*, Editions du Musée Rodin, 2006.

[4] Frederic V. Grunfeld, *Rodin - A Biography*, 1987.

[5] Christina Buley-Uribe, *Rodin and the Cambodian Dancers*, Editions du Musée Rodin, 2006.

Rodin's images of Cambodian dancers, sketched with graphite, coloured with wash in watercolour or gouache on cream vellum paper. A sense of movement is created by not following the drawn lines exactly. 1906.

CHAPTER 5　LATE FRENCH PROTECTORATE

"There is a dignity accumulated through hundreds and hundreds of years, an aristocracy bred by countless generations of court life and adherence to strict and sacred traditions, a tragic evanescence as of a flower which blooms only for a night, to fade at dawn. Even all of these points when thoroughly considered and added to the sum total do not explain the magic quality of these living goddesses."
Ted Shawn on Cambodian dancers.

Following this momentous visit, King Sisowath did little to enhance the status of the dancers, although they had an excellent teacher, Khun Chom Bosseba, a wife of former king Norodom and the mother of Prince Sutharot, who had been with the dancers in France. There are also magical photographs of the dancers taken a few years later, in 1921, by Léon Busy, a former army officer, for the French philanthropist Albert Kahn. These were commissioned by Kahn for his Archives of the Planet, a project to foster peace and understanding throughout the world by sending photographers to capture images of remote cultures.

The autochromes, a colour process where starch grains dyed green, red and blue were stuck to a glass plate, laminated, coated with a panchromatic silver bromide solution and exposed in the camera, resulted in painterly, ethereal qualities that captured the richness of the dancers' costumes and settings. These images are a unique testimony to a rarefied art form of a society in transition. In 1925 the American Burton Holmes, the most celebrated travel photographer and lecturer of his time, also captured enchanting images of the dancers at Angkor.

In spite of this interest, the impetus of dance at the royal court was waning and it was left to Princess Soumphady to look after the children of the dance troupe while King Sisowath, succumbing to his opium addiction, descended into a sad condition, his eyesight failing, wandering uncertainly around the palace

Dancer in prince costume, Royal Palace, Phnom Penh, March 1921. Musée Albert Kahn.

Dancers at Angkor Wat, 1921. Musée Albert Kahn.

Dancers on the causeway, Angkor Wat, c. 1950.
Halton-Deutsche Collection/Corbis.

The Royal Cambodian dancing girls being presented with their
jewels, May 1923. Bettmann Archive.

The Dance of Loyalty to the King, May 1923. Bettmann Archive.

Royal dancers at Angkor Wat. Bettmann Archive.

The dancers of the King of Cambodia, *L'Illustration*, 2 June 1906.
Rodin and the Cambodian dancers.

Above right and right: **Cambodian royal dancers.**
Hulton-Deutsche Collection/Corbis.

grounds wearing only a *krama*. He died in 1927. After his son Monivong (1927-1941) succeeded him, a monarch also amenable to the French rulers, the dance troupe numbered even fewer members. But it was a study of the dance by the French painter and artist George Groslier, who wrote lyrical descriptions, illustrated with his drawings, that helped bring about a resurgence in its importance.

George Groslier

Groslier, who was born in Phnom Penh in 1887, the first child of French parents in the colonial regime, was educated in France but returned to Cambodia where he lived for the rest of his life. He would die tragically, and in mysterious circumstances, under torture by the Japanese Kampetai in Phnom Penh in 1945. During his distinguished career he became Artistic Director under the French administration and created the School of Cambodian Arts and the National Museum, then called the Musée Albert Sarrault after the governor, its design inspired by the graceful Buddhist styles of Khmer architecture.

Groslier, rather alarmingly, stated that dance was dying out, noting that in 1928 there were only eight prima ballerinas, 70 dancers and 40 girls in training, with dancers selling their jewellery and allowing their costumes to fall to pieces. He felt that the colonial authorities were ignoring dance, the living art of the present, to concentrate on the past glories of Angkor. To counteract this, he highlighted the dancers' artistic connection to the bas-reliefs of Angkor[1].

While there is debate among scholars about the extent to which a 'tradition' of Cambodian dance was fostered by Groslier and the French, historicising the court dance as a part of the Angkorean era, itself idealised during the colonial period, this appreciation increased its inherent value. Today, ironically, the role of dancers is once more in the process of re-evaluation as their image is used as one of the 'traditions' of Cambodia to promote tourism (see Chapter 12). But just as the discovery of Angkor and appreciation of dance in the 19th century gave Cambodians a new-found sense of pride and nationalism, so the restoration of Angkor and revival of dance in the 21st century gives back a sense of the nation's soul after the destruction of the Pol Pot regime. In both instances, Cambodia's artistic history takes on a dual aspect, promoting

National Museum designed by George Groslier.

colonialism or tourism while at the same time trying to formulate and preserve its own integrity.

Groslier pleaded for support for the dancers and, as a result, the palace administration and French authorities placed the troupe under the aegis of the Ecole des Beaux Arts, transforming the status of dancers to civil servants. This enabled them to continue, helped not only by Groslier's writings but those of other French visitors such as André Malraux. The author and politician had praised the subtlety of the movements on seeing them perform in 1923 during his visit to Cambodia – when he also attempted to steal a *devata* from the temple of Banteay Srei. Another member of the French administration, Roland Meyer, also wrote in considerable detail about the dance in a semi-autobiographical novel[2], in which the protagonist, an impoverished Frenchman, marries a Cambodian court dancer.

Groslier was among the first to make any kind of written record of the movements of dance[3]. He claimed that there were no fewer than 1,065 principal dance steps and that in this complex form of dance nothing was improvised. Illustrating his theories with delicate drawings, he described the dancers – rather fancifully – as "virginal idols of a gentle and pure people," their dances naïve, like those of children from a bygone age. Appearing in their mask-like white makeup, the colour of purity, of the lotus and the moon, the dancers were ethereal, like goddesses or dolls. Their gestures were "full of nobility and serenity," even though their costumes, especially the intricate golden head-dresses, almost restricted their movements. He was filled with admiration for their hands, describing them as jewels, drawing in detail the bangles, bracelets and rings with which they were adorned. In conclusion, he lamented those hurried

travellers who dismissed the dances as too monoto-
nous and obscure, who never realised that "the gestures .... were caresses." His son, Bernard-Philippe,
who became a curator at Angkor, also shared his
father's enthusiasm for the dancers, describing "the
exquisite sweetness of their expressions the rhythmic
quality of their gestures, the whimsical charm of their
braided hairstyles and of their gilded tiaras."

Groslier's observations went deeper than romantic
impressions, showing also the reality of the dancers' se-
questered lives at the court, revealing that behind the
glamorous exterior they lived almost like prisoners.
The dancers, brought to the palace as little girls at the
age of six years old, the most beautiful and the whitest-
skinned of their villages, would become part of the
king's harem and were never allowed to leave the confines of the palace. King Norodom had been adamant
on this, although King Sisowath had been more le-
nient, allowing them to go out for several days at a
time. For the most part, they lived in a hermetic, seg-
regated world filled with intrigue, jealousy, gossip and
favouritism. Eunuchs were not necessary since no man
was ever allowed into the harem. Groslier described
their modest possessions and humble living quarters,
rows of attached rooms made from wood or brick, improved only if they became one of the king's favourites
or bore him children (the palace compound had its
own maternity quarters), when they would then have a
separate little house. "The poor little solitary princess,"
he surmised, "dreams of having a husband…"

Groslier's views may not have been entirely accurate, however. Groslier and Meyer have both been
criticised as conjuring up an inverted dreamworld[4], a
colonial utopia where the heroes were Frenchmen and
the colonised were Cambodian women hungry for
male domination. Reports by contemporaries, such as
Sappho Marchal[5], showed that, on the contrary, the
dancers had not been abandoned by the king. But
once they had a taste of freedom, they were inclined to
leave the palace, and after some of them married they
found they were unable to return to the old traditions,
especially after they had participated at the Saigon
Exhibition of 1927-28. At this historic exhibition, their
chief guardian apparently stole a number of treasures[6]
which had been entrusted to him by the king and fled
to Thailand, prompting the Royal Palace to reassert
tighter control over the dancers again.

By now the Royal Ballet was reduced to a troupe of
12 dancers and in 1931, when the French government
invited the ballet to another Colonial Exhibition in
Paris, they turned down the invitation. The dance
troupe had divided and a breakaway troupe had been
formed by Princess Say Sangvann, a court favourite
who had married one of the brothers of the king,
Prince Vong Kath. The rift had caused embarrassment
for the French, as the fame of the dancers was such
that all distinguished visitors to Cambodia were eager
to see them. The authorities could not simply ask the
king to put on a performance since the dancers were
part of the royal household rather than mere entertainers. Princess Say Sangvann, however, was willing to
perform for their various events and the French lent
her their support to maintain and train a troupe. She
then took them to France in 1931, in place of the
king's dancers, where they were fêted as much as they
had been in 1906. Cambodia figured prominently at
the Colonial Exhibition with huge, life-size models of
the temples of Angkor which created a surge of
'Angkormania'.

But this severing of links with the royal court
heralded a decline of dance as an ancient spiritual
symbol of a powerful monarch. It placed dancers in
the political arena, as pawns of the French, their status
reduced to that of entertainers, with the king forced to
make compromises to his colonial masters.

Life-size models of Angkor at the Colonial Exhibition, 1931, created a surge of Angkormania in France.

Xenia Zarina: Classic Dances of the Orient

The divided loyalties of these two troupes were vividly described by the Belgian dancer Xenia Zarina[7], who had previously performed with the legendary Russian Michel Fokine whose choreography had re-ignited the creative momentum of Western classical ballet. She came to Phnom Penh and studied under Say Sangvann in 1937, an arrangement made possible through George Groslier when he was director of the Musée Albert Sarrault. Her book is another invaluable record of dance at this time of change and transition.

Zarina observed that the new arrangement offered security for Princess Say Sangvann, giving new stimulus to Cambodian dance, as well as providing satisfaction for visitors and the opportunity for a foreigner to learn more about this exquisite art. "But for this happy circumstance," she writes, "I would have had the utmost difficult in studying Cambodian dance." Say Sangvann was based in Phnom Penh and would then travel to Angkor for performances when invited. Zarina protests in an amusing way about the consequent irregularity of her lessons. "Often I would go on the appointed day only to find that the Princess and the whole ballet had vanished. The servant did not speak any French and explained to me by waving his hands in the air. Presumably the ballet had flown off to other regions, like the carved *apsarases* at Angkor where the whole ballets soar joyously across the skies. Then suddenly the Princess and ballet would reappear and my lessons would continue."

She praised the teaching and concluded that performances outside the palace were a necessary sign of the times but lamented that the king was reduced to petty squabbles about funds and costumes. She noted that in 1937 for the Royal Ballet a prince's costume cost about 8,000 *piastres* ($2,000) and a princess's costume cost about 5,000 *piastres* ($1,250). The crowns, *mkots*, and jewels were set in pure gold for the leading roles of the Royal Ballet, although other ballets could not afford more than silver gilt for the leading roles. She recorded that the Royal Ballet was composed of eight ballet mistresses, 108 dancers, two comic mimes, two singing teachers, two first singers, two readers, 24 choristers, 12 dressers, four guardians of jewels and costumes, nine males musicians and two conductors.

Among those she befriended was Samdach Chaufea Thiounn, the prime minister and the first

Above left: **Xenia Zarina posing as an** *apsara*.

Above: **Xenia in the costume of classical Cambodian dance.**

Cambodian to write on dance. He produced a charming publication, *Danses Cambodgiennes*, illustrated by Sappho Marchal. In it he writes that the head-dress was the most expensive part of the costume, costing 800 piastres, and combined with the jewellery was worth 2,000 piastres

Zarina's description of the training includes captivating details such as the fact that early morning dew was collected from plants in the palace gardens to massage all the joints of the little ballerinas, from wrists to toes. She describes the prayer that is a salute to the teachers, the *Sampeah Kru*, complete with offerings of betel leaves, candles, incense sticks, perfumed water and bouquets of flowers as offerings. The sacred ceremonies continued unabated in spite of the changes to the status of dance.

She confirms Groslier's description of the dancers more or less incarcerated in the palace, although some of the royal dancers would be allowed out to go shopping. "While not dancing or rehearsing they ..... sew pure gold beans in ancient patterns onto velvet for new scarf capes. ....When a dancer becomes old or incapacitated, she may retire, or remain as teacher or wardrobe mistress"

Ted Shawn as Shiva Nataraja.

Ruth St Denis in oriental dance costume.

Ruth St Denis as Hindu dancer, Radha.

Of special note is her description of the annual Water Festival on the Mekong river, the *Fêtes des Eaux*, held when the waters of the river reverse their flow at the height of the rainy season, backing up into the Tonle Sap lake. Zarina vividly described the fireworks and festivities that lasted a whole week.

"At the *Fêtes des Eaux*, at the Mekong river … astronomers know what and what hour this phenomenon will occur, and as the life of Cambodia is intimately connected with the Mekong, everyone takes part in the traditional celebrations, which last a whole week. … The King changes his residence from the pink walled palace to the royal houseboat on the river. In a procession of elephants in elaborate trappings, beflowered motorcars and decorated officials, His Majesty is carried on a golden throne on a gold lacquered platform borne on the shoulders of many servitors. High over the King is carried the traditional golden parasol, symbol of royalty and sanctity since ancient times throughout the East. The sculptured kings of Angkor have identical parasols over their precious heads."

"In a spacious pavilion beside the famous silver pagoda, provincial ballets requested for the festivities dance all day. They danced their very best, for if they pleased some palace talent scout they might be chosen for the King's ballet, which would be a great honour and their families would be well provided for ever after. There appeared to be quite a large membership in the ballets I saw, and in certain scenes representing processions or a trip to another locality, the whole troupe took part following the leading dancers, getting smaller and younger and less adept and less well costumed until the last tiny tots stumbingly brought up the rear, practically in rags, and doing their best not to forget the dance figures."

Ted Shawn, Gods Who Dance

As international interest in Cambodian dance grew, Groslier's book in particular was to inspire not only his fellow countrymen but dance practitioners in America. Ted Shawn (1891-1972), one of America's pioneering dancers and choreographers, who believed implicitly that dance was a form of religious expression, was so fascinated by Groslier's descriptions that when he travelled to Asia in 1925 to study dance, he made a special trip to Cambodia, recorded in his book *Gods Who Dance*.

It includes his impression of a visit to the Royal Palace "an Oriental fairyland … the architecture so slight and exquisitely graceful …". He was enchanted as the floor was suddenly filled with dancers. "They were like live jewels frosted with gold," he wrote. "Vibrant, rich and satisfying colour, the fire of priceless jewels, the overpowering scent of jasmine and champak blossoms which hung in tassels from their crowns, and were woven into bracelets for their arms. Twenty exquisitely beautiful girls, half of them dressed as princesses and half as princes, danced in two long lines down the floor. As I watched, I realized why no words, written or spoken could ever recreate this scene, for a simultaneous attack was made through all the senses at once – even the moving picture, perfectly synchronized with the perfectly recorded music, would still be unable to give the caress of the tropic breeze which bore heavy scented perfumes of musk and jasmine."

Shawn's wife, the dancer Ruth St Denis, also believed in the sanctity of dance, turning to the Orient for inspiration and learning Hindu movements. "Anyone who dances is momentarily in harmony with the great cosmic order of the universe," she wrote. Recalling photographs she had seen at an East Indian sideshow at the fairground of Coney Island, she choreographed a dance based on Hindu mythology, Radha, in 1906. Rodin also drew her. Shawn and St Denis were among the greatest influences on American dance and at their school, Denishawn, pupils included Martha Graham, who would dominate Western dance until her death in 1991. "If the dancing of any one country is truly great," wrote Shawn, "it must have been founded on principles which are true everywhere, and thus the study of these principles is of value to the dancers of every country."

St Denis and Shawn were intrigued by the artistic reserve so characteristic of the Cambodian dances and drama. Whenever desire or passion is depicted, Shawn noted that "it is portrayed with so much restraint as to be hardly recognizable. Many Oriental gestures, meaning nothing whatsoever to us, have suggestions of burning love to them … of course the fact that the Cambodian dancers are all women, and have been for centuries, has made lovemaking in the dances a thing of symbolism rather than actuality."

He was struck by the "ceaseless and unchanging" rhythm of Cambodian music, which gives a "sense of monotony" to the dance, a quality often remarked upon. However, he observed, "this monotony is only a surface impression, for when one begins to look for variety of steps and gestures one finds more than one expects." He noted especially "the wonder and beauty of the arm and hand movements" and the legs always in *plié*.

The charm and the essence of this dancing, he said, eludes description. "The color, gold and jewels of the costume, the perfume of the jasmine blossoms they wear, borne on the warm breezes of the tropic night, the hypnotic rhythm of the gongs … the fragile beauty of the dancers, the serpent-supple arms and hands, all combined cannot contain the secret of their power. There is a dignity accumulated through hundreds and hundreds of years, an aristocracy bred by countless generations of court life and adherence to strict and sacred traditions, a tragic evanescence as of a flower which blooms only for a night, to fade at dawn. Even all of these points when thoroughly considered and added to the sum total do not explain the magic quality of these living goddesses."

Shawn's affinity with Cambodian dance arose from his own conviction that dancing was driven by religious beliefs. "I could not conceive of God being without rhythm, with grace, without intelligent expression, nor without possession of infinite forms of beauty through which to express His infinite Rhythmic Being. Even so it came somewhat as a shock when I definitely agreed within myself that mine was a God who dances – for in spite of everything there still clings to the word 'dance' so many associations of triviality and sensuality. However, I found new concepts of the dance when I viewed it in the light of God's activity, and that dancing could be truly great only when it was Infinite Rhythm, Infinite Beauty, Infinite Strength, Lightness, Speed, Grace and Intelligence, finding outlet through the channel of a human dancer."

The dancers who embodied that infinite rhythm and beauty had become, as Shawn had observed, not only objects of desire but subjects of study all over the world. But even as he was publicising the magical and sacred dimension of Cambodian dance, it was once more on the verge of disappearing.

Ted Shawn as Rama.

[1] George Groslier, *Danseuses cambodgiennes anciennes et modernes*, 1929.

[2] Roland Meyer, *Saramani, danseuse khmèr*, 1922.

[3] George Groslier, *Le Theatre et La Danse au Cambodge*, 1929.

[4] Sappho Marchal, *La Danse du Cambodge* and *Khmer Costumes and Ornaments of the Devatas of Angkor Wat*, 1927.

[5] Womanising Indochina: Colonial Cambodia' Penny Edwards from *Domesticating the Empire*, Julia Clancy-Smith and Frances Gouda, 2007.

[6] Julio Jeldres *The Royal House of Cambodia*.

[7] Xenia Zarina, Royal Cambodian Dances, *Classic Dances of the Orient*, 1967.

"O body swayed to music, O brightening glance,
How can we know the dancer from the dance?"
William Butler Yeats.

The influence of Khmer and Siamese dance was everywhere in the early 20th century. Far Eastern art was the rage, with collectors like Emile Guimet and Henri Cernuschi bringing back artefacts to France that would become museum collections. The visit of the Cambodian dancers to the West inspired a thirst for exoticism and Orientalism. Dancers like Mata Hari, a Dutchwoman who renamed herself after visiting Java (her stage name meant 'sunrise'), performed an Oriental dance at the Musée Guimet of Asiatic Arts in Paris, before going on to more nefarious activities such as espionage. Ruth St Denis performed a Hindu dance at the Théâtre Marigny in 1906. Even the dazzling Russian dancer Vaslav Nijinksy performed a Siamese dance, Les Orientales, at the Paris Opera in 1910. Described as looking like an oriental god, as his fingers "bending and coiling, created a pattern as if to entwine the angular and plastic lines of the slow dance," he was photographed in his exotic costume in the garden of the artist Jacques-Emile Blanche. Yet, in spite of this surge in interest internationally, Cambodia's Royal Ballet seemed to be on the decline.

Above and below: **Nijinksy in Les Orientales, St Petersburg State Theatre Archives.**

Queen Kossamak and the dance

But it was at this time that Khun Meak, a former star of the Royal Ballet during the reign of King Sisowath, and one of his mistresses, began teaching a small group of girls in an endeavour to re-establish the purity of Khmer classical dance. At her suggestion, the troupe came under the tutelage of Princess Sisowath Kossamak. Daughter of King Monivong, the princess, who would eventually become queen when her son Norodom Sihanouk relinquished his crown, became a patron of the ballet although she was not herself a dancer. This was the turning point because with her tremendous energy, dedication and imagination,

Queen Kossamak.

Princess Kossamak not only rekindled a dying art but reformulated it for the 20th century. Cambodian dance was elevated to new heights.

After the death of King Monivong in 1941, the French *Resident Superieur* had informed Princess Kossamak that the ballet would have to be sacrificed in order to save 600 *riels* a month for its upkeep. But Sihanouk, who had been crowned in the April, aged only 19 years old, immediately donated a monthly

Norodom Sihanouk.

Norodom Sihanouk – Patron of the dance

That Sihanouk was knowledgeable on dance is evident from the record of a visit in 1948 by the British Commissioner for Southeast Asia, the Right Honourable Malcolm MacDonald. He described[1] how he was a guest of the king at a performance in the Chanchaya Pavilion, recalling a magical experience, under a night sky of "velvety black where myriads of stars jewelled the heavens." He marvelled at the dance costumes, likening the head-dresses to a medieval knight's helmet, wrought in gold and inset with precious stones. "Always their splendid costumes gave dramatic dignity to their actions, and the stepping of the dancers was in conforming with this stately mood. There is nothing spontaneous, nothing free – still less abandoned – about Cambodian dancing. All the movements are restrained by custom, confined within bounds set with formal precision by centuries of tradition." Sensitive to the nuances of the art form, he understood its significance and context. "They pass through a ceaseless succession of gesticulations, every one of which has a symbolism well known to the tutored Cambodian audience," he wrote. But, remarking on the lack of facial emotion, he concluded wryly: "Thus the performance proceeds with as much stiff precision as the drill of a platoon of soldiers on parade."

The theory that Siamese dance was influenced by Khmer dance is reinforced by MacDonald who was told by King Sihanouk how the Royal Corps de Ballet had been left behind when the Siamese captured Angkor and that they were taken to the court of Ayutthaya. The Khmer dance tradition was introduced to Siam, claimed the king, and in turn the palace tailors clothed the foreign ballerinas in rich raiment of Siamese style. When, many years later, the dancers returned to Phnom Penh and dancing was revived, the ballets were the old ones hallowed over centuries, but the clothing was imported from Siam. Sihanouk's references support the accepted, although disputed, historical background of Khmer and Siamese influences. During his reign, and under Queen Kossamak's patronage, Thai influences were gradually phased out as the dance was reinvigorated with a more Khmer style.

Sihanouk was a patron of the arts from the start, alternating his political activities with his many other, less regal, interests such as jazz and film-making. Having crusaded for independence from the French, he succeeded in November 1953 in freeing Cambodia

Dancers from the Royal Court, Fonds Iconographiques Mission des Etrangères.

allowance and provided living quarters for the dancers. In November 1942, a magnificent performance was staged for the visit of the Emperor Bao Dai of Vietnam. For this historic occasion, although the French authorities still supported Say Sangvann's private troupe, King Sihanouk arranged a special presentation of his royal dancers on his birthday for the Emperor. It won over the French who could see that the royal troupe, under Queen Kossamak, was better than Say Sangvann's. From then onwards, the Royal Ballet became the undisputed repository of Khmer classical dancing.

By the time Sihanouk renounced his throne to became Head of State in 1954, retaining the title of 'Prince', the dancers, who accompanied him everywhere, were like his ambassadors, reprising the status they had had at the height of the Khmer empire. Few rulers could have boasted a more enchanting or alluring entourage, domestically and internationally, than Sihanouk and his dancers.

Queen Kossamak with Jacqueline
Kennedy and Sihanouk, 1967.
From *The Royal House of Cambodia* by
Julio Jeldres.

from almost a century of colonial rule. When he abdicated the throne in 1954 to become Head of State, taking on a political role that the constitution restricted him from assuming as monarch, he made his father, Norodom Suramarit, king instead and Princess Kossamak became Queen Sisowath Kossamak Nearireat, the Queen Mother.

Because Sihanouk was revered by many Cambodians as a sort of god-king, invested with the aura of his forebears, the *devarajas*, he was still regarded as the king, sometimes referring to the Cambodians as his children. Under his *Sangkum Reastr Niyum*, People's Socialist Community (1955-1970), the country experienced something of a 'golden age.' William Shawcross[2] cites the many journalists, diplomats and tourists who visited at the time, whose impression of Cambodia was of an "an idyllic, antique land unsullied by the brutalities of the modern world." Although this was to prove ultimately illusory, it was nevertheless a buoyant period, with dynamic economic growth and cultural prosperity.

The Queen Mother assembled all the former teachers to help in reforming the Royal Ballet. Glittering gold and diamond costumes were created. Thousands of girls were taught to dance. Anyone could come to the palace rehearsal rooms to participate in the workouts and the Queen Mother would often spot young talent in this way. She understood both the political and spiritual importance of the royal ballet and, without losing the essence of their sacred nature, performances were shortened to a more manageable two hours, with an opening piece, a dramatic section and a finale, which was perfect for diplomatic occasions. Some pieces were just 15 minutes long. The *Reamker*, which often lasted all night, was rearranged into shorter sequences. She enhanced the theatrical dimension, emulating European staging techniques. The dance *Tep Monoram*, for example, was transformed from a duet of prince and princess to a grander piece for 12 dancers performing in close synchronicity. She brought male dancers into the company, focusing especially on the monkey roles, from the *Reamker*, whose mischievous humour and acrobatic talents have delighted audiences ever since.

Until Sihanouk's reign classical culture had been the preserve of religion and then royalty. Now it expanded beyond the confines of the palace and was placed on a wider national and international stage, while other performing arts such as *lakhon yike* and

lakhon bassac became popular among new audiences. Subsidised productions in the capital and throughout the regions thrived and private companies run by impresarios were set up for profit.

Sihanouk regarded performing culture as part of national prestige as well as a court ritual. Under the queen's direction, the ballet was reinstated as an honoured institution, and the *lakhon kbach boran* became an important attribute of the king's power again.

In 1962 the Royal Ballet was given an administrative status similar to national troupes in Europe, such as the Royal Ballet of Great Britain. It numbered 284 members, including one star dancer, five *premieres danseuses*, 25 *corps de ballet*, four clowns, 160 students, 17 dance mistresses, two male dance teachers, 10 singers and rhythm keepers, 24 musicians, six music students, 14 dressers and makeup artists, four seamstresses, six apprentice seamstresses and six jewellery keepers.[3] The Royal Ballet School offered 'voluntary, classes to 460 students on a daily basis. Unlike their predecessors at the court, dancers were now free to marry and live away from the palace.

On 25 November 1964 the Royal University of Fine Arts was established, comprising five faculties: choreographic arts, music, fine art, archaeology, architecture and city planning. The first rector was His Excellency Vann Molyvann (b. 1926), eminent architect and prominent figure in Cambodian culture, who designed many of the capital's public buildings and monuments at this time. A National Conservatory for Performing Arts ensured the preservation and restaging of all forms of Cambodian performing arts. Ballet masters were recruited by the Conservatory and were given the stability of civil servant status. In 1966 Sihanouk gave the dancers their own theatre in Phnom Penh, the Preah Suramarit Theatre, usually known as the Tonle Bassac Theatre, named after the nearby river. It symbolised the new, modern Cambodia, where art had its own special place in the city, just as theatres and opera houses in France had become the centrepieces of cities.

HRH Princess Buppha Devi aged 5 with Ms. Yat.

Princess Norodom Buppha Devi

Among Queen Kossamak's many outstanding achievements was the training of Sihanouk's graceful daughter, Her Royal Highness Princess Norodom Buppha Devi, who became the greatest dancer of her generation. Princess Buppha Devi was born in 1943 to one of the king's court dancers, Neak Moneang Phat Kanhol. Of Sihanouk's 14 children, by five wives, several others were dancers, including Norodom Sihamoni who was also a choreographer, (see Chapter 7), and Norodom Chakrapong who danced the role of Hanuman in the *Reamker*. Princess Buppha Devi started dancing at five years old. By the age of 15 she was the shining star of the Royal Ballet and at 18 was granted the title of Prima Ballerina.

When Princess Buppha Devi granted me an interview in 2006 she told me how her training had even included studying sculptures at Angkor, so closely associated was dance with the temples. On a more lighthearted note, she also recalled how she took dance lessons with her five sisters, among whom was Princess Sorya Roeungsey who did not have the right physique for a dancer. The princess laughed as she remembered the king's reaction to the hapless princess's endeavours: "My father said to her after a performance, 'I will pay you *not* to dance'." The requirement for a perfect dancer, said the princess, was to be 1m 50cm tall, slender and fine boned. These were all attributes that

HRH Princess Buppha Devi. Photo: Loke Wan Tho from *Angkor*, Malcolm MacDonald, 1957.

HRH Princess Buppha Devi. From *The Royal House of Cambodia* by Julio Jeldres.

Middle and right: **HRH Princess Buppha Devi**.

she possessed, along with a natural grace and delicacy that made her performances so legendary.

The princess was raised by her grandparents and visited her father only on weekends. Living with Queen Kossamak, she was surrounded by dancers, and taught by Khun Meak as well as other great masters such as Mam Pong and Mam Yim Yan, the grandmother of Proeung Chhieng, now dean of choreography. She learned four main roles and more than a thousand gestures of the repertoire.

Buppha Devi danced only at the court, as was the custom, rather than for the public, and on special visits abroad with the king. She danced for President Eisenhower in America in 1960, and for many august visitors to Cambodia, especially Britain's Princess Margaret and Lord Snowden in 1963 at the Chaktomuk Theatre (the gift of a cigar box from King Sihanouk to Princess Margaret and her husband was sold with all Princess Margaret's effects in 2006 at Christie's) and the Duke and Duchess of Kent. She captivated General Tito, Jawaharlal Nehru, Premier Zhou Enlai and President Sukarno (who was apparently so enamoured of her that he asked Sihanouk for her hand in marriage), as well as General de Gaulle, at the Opéra in Paris in 1964, and in Cambodia when

he visited in 1966, and Jackie Kennedy during her well publicised visit in 1967. The princess performed on the terrace of Angkor Wat, an event recalled by Sihanouk in his memoirs: "One of the highlights of the de Gaulles' stay was a visit to the temples of Angkor and the spectacular *son et lumière* I arranged in the venerable setting of Angkor Wat, the magnificence of which had never been seen before. De Gaulle was spellbound by the fireworks and by the performances which followed." Indeed, these performances, by candlelight, on the causeway of the temple, must have been utterly magical to watch and to perform.

Queen Kossamak choreographed dances especially for Buppha Devi. The Apsara Dance, or *Robam Apsara*, now one of the most popular in the repertoire, a graceful composition of sinuous hand gestures and sensuous body movements, was created in 1962. The princess became the symbol of classical Khmer dance in this role. Even though, as she herself points out, it is not a classical role, it has come to be regarded as one, especially abroad. In particular, her beautiful hands, with their long, slim fingers, bent right back with extraordinary suppleness, move slowly and eloquently through the gestures of dance with a refinement that is awe inspiring. She embodied Cambodian dance at its acme.

Princess Buppha Devi and Norodom Sihanouk with General and Mme de Gaulle, Paris Opera, 1964.

Left: **Princess Buppha Devi dancing on stage at the Opera de Paris, 1964.**

Prince Norodom Sihanouk was highly revered by many Cambodians.

General Lon Nol.

As the music starts, five *apsaras* are represented on a bas-relief, and, like a dream, come slowly to life, descending from the niches to re-enact a traditional dance of salutation. As they conclude their beguiling dance, the dream fades and the five *apsaras* return to their niches in the stone temple. In this piece, Queen Kossamak carefully recreated the same golden *mkot*, ornate jewellery and stylised hand gestures of the *apsaras* at Angkor Wat, adding the shimmering, close fitting cream silk costume. Buppha Devi also starred in the title role of a film called *Apsara*, made by Sihanouk, who made many films during his reign that starred several of his 14 children. Queen Kossomak and Princess Buppha Devi brought classical dance to the world but also, more importantly, to ordinary Cambodian people, for the first time. Previously, it had been performed only for royalty, to honour their ancestors, but now it entered the public domain.

Decline of the golden age

The creativity and glamour of these years was not to last, however. The era was marred by internal political problems, uprisings and plots to overthrow Sihanouk, less revered in the city than the countryside. Although a Buddhist, his rule was violent. As William Shawcross writes: "Like any other country, Cambodia was the complex product of geographical, social and political experience that provides precedent and warning for future history. It was never quite the smiling, gentle land that foreigners liked to see."[3]

Within the country, French educated intellectuals, including Saloth Sar, who would later become Pol Pot, and his colleagues Khieu Sampan and Ieng Sary, who had studied Marxism, Trotskyism and Maoism, were organising communist guerilla armies – nicknamed *Les Khmers Rouges* by Sihanouk. By the mid-1960s, Sihanouk's rule was jeapardised by the Vietnam War which would change the course of his country's history. In March 1969, President Richard Nixon ordered the bombing of communist sanctuaries in eastern Cambodia, on the borders of Vietnam, driving the Vietnamese further inside Cambodia. This bombing turned young, disaffected people of peasant backgrounds into revolutionaries and although initially a small army, the Khmer Rouge's numbers doubled during this time. Although Sihanouk steered Cambodia through a policy of neutrality, the United States and North Vietnam were waging war on Cambodian soil. As Sihanouk's neutralists policies disintegrated, he was ousted in 1970 while on a visit to Beijing in an American-backed *coup d'etat* by his prime minister, General Lon Nol, and deputy, Prince Sisowath Sirik Matak.

During Lon Nol's ensuing Khmer Republic (1970-1975) the dancers were forced to relinquish their royal status to become a national dance troupe. Nevertheless they had a successful tour to America in 1971, performing at the Brooklyn Academy of Music in an Afro-Asian dance festival. However, as chaos and civil war enveloped Cambodia, the arts were dismissed as part of an antiquated feudal social system. Dancers soon dispersed and jewellery and costumes disappeared. By 1975, those dancers who continued classes and rehearsals were frightened away by attacks on the city. Rockets were falling almost hourly and one injured a dancer in the palace grounds. Queen Kossamak was placed under house arrest. Prince Souvanna Phouma of Laos offered asylum, but this was discouraged. She was eventually freed following the intervention of Zhou Enlai and Richard Nixon, and allowed to leave Cambodia in 1973 with Princess Buppha Devi for Canton. Queen Kossamak died in Beijing on 27 April 1975.

Buppha Devi would not return to Cambodia until 1991. She spent much of that time in Paris where she met refugee dancers and musicians. She taught young dancers and in 1982 travelled to refugee camps on the Thai-Cambodian border to teach dance.

Far left: **Pol Pot.**

Princess Buppha Devi
teaching Cambodian
refugees in Thai camps.
From *The Royal House of
Cambodia* by Julio Jeldres.

During the Lon Nol regime, Cambodia suffered more intense bombardment by American B-52s which dropped half a million tons of bombs along the country's borders with Vietnam to destroy the Viet Cong, resulting in the deaths of about 600,000 Cambodian people. Cambodia became known as the 'sideshow' to the Vietnam war. The Khmer Rouge were growing in strength, garnering support in the beleaguered countryside, attacking government forces and cutting off their supply routes. Rural disenchantment with the Lon Nol government and the fact that it was backed by the US and had ousted Sihanouk were determining factors in allegiance to the anti-imperialist, anti-colonialist Khmer Rouge. They appealed to notions of nationalism as well as communism, whose theories were little understood by ordinary Cambodians.

By 1975, after American forces had finally quit Vietnam, the Lon Nol republic, riddled with corruption, started to collapse. By January, roads were cut to Phnom Penh, a city that, swollen with refugees, had gone from 600,000 to 2 million people, and the rebel forces started their bombardment. In April, Lon Nol escaped into exile. Foreign diplomats and aides were hastily airlifted out by helicopters as the Khmer Rouge army started to advance on the city. When they seized power on 17 April 1975, dancing, music and all of life as it had been lived hitherto came to a halt.

Sun setting behind the Royal Palace.

[1] Malcolm MacDonald, *Angkor*, 1958.

[2] William Shawcross, *Sideshow*, 1979.

[3] William Shawcross, *Sideshow*, 1979.

CHAPTER 7 POL POT REGIME: DANCE WITH DEATH

Khmer Rouge enter Phnom Penh.

Young Khmer Rouge soldiers.

"Keeping you is no gain; losing you is no loss."
Khmer Rouge dictum.

On the morning of 17 April 1975, the Khmer Rouge, the guerilla army trained by Pol Pot, marched silently into Phnom Penh. A rag-tag army of teenage boys, dressed in black pyjamas with red cotton *kramas*, they were initially greeted with flowers and white flags by a population who thought the war had ended. But the euphoria was short-lived. The soldiers immediately ordered everyone to leave the city, evacuating two million people in three days, many of whom were refugees from the bombing, and then executed all those connected with the fallen Lon Nol government. "The first act of Khmer Rouge Rule," writes William Shawcross[1] "the instant evacuation of Phnom Penh and other towns in April 1975 symbolised its absolute nature."

The troops concentrated first on ordering the wounded from hospitals, then went from house to house, forcing people to leave. Everybody was marched out into the countryside, many dying on the way. In the ensuing bloodbath, all educated people were murdered, including doctors, nurses, dentists, teachers, lawyers, intellectuals and artists. Anybody who spoke a foreign language and even those who wore glasses were instantly executed. Announcements were made that dancers were to register with the new authorities. Ninety percent of the performers and musicians who did so were killed. Those who did manage to survive tried to hide all evidence of their professions, learning to say nothing and concealing their knowledge and backgrounds.

The country was renamed Democratic Kampuchea. The party was ruled by Saloth Sar, who renamed himself Pol Pot and conceived one of the most fanatical social revolutions in history, called Year Zero. The clock would be turned back to the beginning, and the country was cut off from the outside world. In his Maoist rural utopia there would be no more art, dance, music, songs, laughter, education, money, laws, religion, health care, family, postal system or telephones. The banks were blown up and the cathedral dismantled. The cities were all systematically emptied. Phnom Penh now lay abandoned, just as Angkor had been in the 15th century, devoid of human beings and reclaimed by tropical vegetation. It was a ghost town. Cambodia's culture was completely destroyed along with all those associated with it, and "two thousand years of Cambodian history ended," as its spokesmen declared. Individualism was replaced by collectivism and co-operatives. Cambodia was turned into a huge forced labour camp where the population lived on collective farms, toiling endlessly on the land on doomed, badly planned agricultural projects, working from dawn to dusk and, during the full moon, most of the night. The Khmer Rouge starved people and many, already debilitated by war, succumbed to disease and death. Arrests were arbitrary, and execution horrific. Torture, as shown in Tuol Sleng, a school turned interrogation centre and now a Museum of Genocide, defied imagination, perpetrated by teenage soldiers who had been indoctrinated with brutality.

Forced labour under the Khmer Rouge.

The dancers, embodiment of the gods, were now plunged into hell. The dancer Sok Chay, in the film *The Tenth Dancer*, broke down in tears as she remembered how they laboured unceasingly in backbreaking work. When they went to sleep there was "no time to rest, no time to dream" as they had to rise again so soon.

Artists were targeted and as rumours spread about corpses of actors and musicians in prisons and torture centres, they buried their costumes and jewellery, burned their old photographs and tried to appear as illiterate peasants, seamstresses or cyclo drivers. Their flawless hands, unmarked by manual labour, would betray them as city people as opposed to peasants and they tried to conceal them. Like the rest of the population, they lived in huts or slept in the open, working in gangs tilling rice fields or hacking down trees in malarial forests, labouring 18 hours a day. One of the first victims of the Khmer Rouge was Hang Thun Hak, former Rector of the University of Fine Arts, who had written about the royal ballet, and who had been a political adviser to Lon Nol. Sinn Sisamouth, a popular classical singer, was immediately executed.

Pol Pot had had close family connections with the Royal Ballet. Born Saloth Sar, the eighth of nine children, he had come to Phnom Penh at the age of six years old to be educated and looked after by relatives. His older sister, Saloth Roeung, known as Saroen, was a dancer at the Royal Palace. She was taught by their cousin, Khun Meak, the former ballet star and favourite mistress of King Sisowath, bearing the king a son named Kossarak. Khun Meak remained a teacher of the *corps de ballet* and paid for some of Pol Pot's education. (She died of starvation under the Khmer Rouge, and one of her daughters, arrested for trying to buy rice, had her breasts slices off and bled to death.) Pol Pot's elder brother, Saloth Suong, also worked in the palace as a clerk in the 1940s and married Chea Samy, a court dancer and teacher, who survived the regime and taught until her death in 1994.

Philip Short[2] writes that the teenage Saloth Sar regularly visited his sister Saroen, who had become one of King Monivong's favourites, and would have gone into the harem, a place "awash with repressed sexuality," influencing a boy "who would spend the rest of his life dissimulating his thoughts behind an impenetrable wreath of smiles and laughter."

After Phnom Penh, Saloth Sar went to university in Paris in 1949, where his future comrades were also educated, including Khieu Sampan. In 1957, Khieu Sampan was photographed in Paris in female costume dancing the role of Seda in the *Reamker* to celebrate the 2,500th anniversary of the birth of the Buddha. Although Saloth Sar stayed again with Saloth Suong in Phnom Penh after his return from France in 1953, once he started his communist activities in the 1960s, he never saw his brother or Chea Samy again. Suong was forced out of the city in the mass evacuation. Saloth Sar's older brother Saloth Chhay also collapsed and died on the march out of Phnom Penh.

So Saloth Sar had grown up among dancers and a refined artistic milieu that adhered to centuries-old traditions which would eventually be the target of his total destruction. As David Chandler writes:[3] "It's easy to imagine Saloth Sar in the 1930s huddled at the edge of the stage watching the masked and powdered dancers, trained by his cousin and perhaps including his sister and his brother's wife, perform by the light of hundreds of candles ..." Chandler speculates that perhaps this tradition of self-concealment, combined with the costumes, role play and empowerment that comes from performing, helped Saloth Sar to shape his public persona. "He was perceived by many throughout his career as 'clean and smooth,' almost as if he were a dancer hiding behind a mask."

Yet, miraculously, Pol Pot did not destroy Angkor, which remained for him the pre-eminent symbol of Cambodia's past splendour, reinforced by a xenophobic belief in the purity of the Khmer race during the

Khieu Sampan dancing Seda.

Pol Pot and his clique at Angkor.

Angkorian empire. In part, this may have accounted for his forming an alliance with Prince Sihanouk, still regarded by most Cambodians as a semi-divine monarch and descendent of the *devarajas*. Sihanouk's return from Beijing in the September as nominal head of the government, and presence during the early stages of the revolution, maintained a sense of patriotism within the country as his overthrow was considered a sacrilege. But Pol Pot, who had remained secretive about his identity, gradually became known in 1976 as the leader of the Democratic Kampuchea.

Dancing *apsara* and bullet holes, Angkor Wat.

Prince Norodom Sihamoni

Sihanouk's son, the dancer and choreographer Prince Norodom Sihamoni, now King of Cambodia, spent the Khmer Rouge years with his father in the Royal Palace. Sihanouk resigned in April 1976 but was kept under palace arrest for almost three years with Queen Monineath and another of their sons, Prince Norindrapong, two of the king's 14 children. The rest escaped abroad, although five perished during the Pol Pot Regime, together with one of Sihanouk's five wives, Mam Manivan Phanivong, a Laotian, who was killed by the Khmer Rouge.

Prince Sihamoni, who was born in 1953, studied in Prague from the age of eight, where he attended the Conservatoire and concentrated on ballet, music, in particular the piano, and theatre, and eventually graduated from the Academy of Performing Arts, Prague. He also studied cinematography in Pyongyan, Korea. He has devoted most of his life to dance, both Cambodian and Western. He briefly described the Khmer Rouge years when I interviewed him in April 1995 in the Royal Palace in Phnom Penh. He had brought a French ballet troupe, Les Jeunes Ballet de France, to the city from Paris, where he had been living since 1982, working as Ambassador, Permanent Representative of Cambodia to UNESCO.

"Many people don't realise that we lost two sisters and three brothers during the war, as well as 11 of their children," said the Prince. "The four of us were imprisoned in the palace, together with three close women friends of my mothers. During that time, we saw no-one. We had no staff, no cooks or gardeners. For food, we grew vegetables and fruit in the garden of the palace. There were banana trees, we had plots, and we grew everything. Twice a week, Khmer Rouge guards came to the back door and gave us rice and fish. We cooked everything ourselves. For our clothes, we wore black clothes, given to us by the Khmer Rouge. We washed everything ourselves."

"If we were ill, my mother treated us. She was marvellous. My mother had been very active in the Cambodian Red Cross, and was Honorary President from 1961, until the Lon Nol coup in 1970. She had a medical kit which she had brought with her from China, and she would look after us. I remember one of the women friends who was with us fell one day and cut open her head badly. My mother went straight to her medical kit and got out instruments and parted her hair like this," – he demonstrated on his own head as he described it – "and cleaned up the wound, which was deep, and sewed it up."

He recalled how they were completely out of contact with the outside world, except that his father listened secretly at night on a small radio to *Voice of America*. That was how they heard about the massacres and about what was going on. But even so they did not know the extent of what was happening beyond the palace. They did not know about Tuol Sleng. His father asked to be let out to visit his country, to see his people, but the Khmer Rouge refused. He said the period was a very unhappy one, "especially for our morale. My father's morale was very low. I got on with things. I am very physical, being a dancer, so I worked in the gardens. I cleaned out the throne hall."

He recollected the one meeting he had had with Pol Pot. "He was like a statue, cold, glacial, unreal. I knew from the beginning that the Khmer Rouge were evil, that they were devils. But many people believed in what the Khmer Rouge were doing. My brother Norindrapong supported them. But at the end of the war, when he saw what had happened, he became psychologically ill. He is still ill, now."

Prince Sihamoni remembered that when the Khmer Rouge heard that the Vietnamese were approaching at the end of 1978, they moved the family from the palace to a nearby colonial villa. (The villa later became a restaurant, Café No Problem, the most popular in the city at the time of the interview). "I remember we were taken through narrow paths amid lots of trees, to a villa where we were shut in. The entire city had become overgrown with vegetation during the three years when it had lain deserted and abandoned."

After the Vietnamese invasion in January 1979 the royal family left on the last Chinese aeroplane to Beijing on January 6th. Sihamoni remained there for two years with his parents, and then went to Pyongyang, Korea, working as his father's secretary. But in 1982, he asked his father if he could go to France, where there were many Cambodian refugees. (He is fluent in French, Czech, English and Russian.) During the next ten years in Paris he became professor of classical dance and artistic pedagogy at the Marius Petipa Conservatory, at the Gabriel Fauré Conservatory and at the W A Mozart Conservatory, and performed and choreographed ballets with a troupe he formed himself called Ballet Deva. They appeared in France, China and Korea. The king also made two ballet films, Four Elements and Dream. Among the dances he choreo-graphed was Duel, created especially for a gala performance that I attended at the Chaktomuk Theatre in Phnom Penh in April 1995 (see Chapter 9).

Meanwhile Prince Norodom Sihanouk would not return to Cambodia until 1991. The Pol Pot regime lasted three years, eight months and 20 days. Through all this time, Angkor, one of the most spiritual places on earth, lay silent and abandoned, while in the countryside Cambodia's people suffered torment and death. At the Vietnamese invasion of January 1979, Pol Pot escaped with his forces to the north-west and Thailand, where he remained hidden until 1997. After being discovered by the American journalist Nate Thayer in the jungle in 1997, and subjected to a 'kangaroo' court hearing, he died on 15 April 1998.

In describing his regime, historian Jean Lacouture coined the word 'autogenocide' to differentiate Pol Pot's murder of his own people from that of other genocidal wars. The population of Cambodia before the Pol Pot regime was 7.4 million. Between one and three million people died of starvation, disease and execution. Subsequently the Vietnamese occupied Cambodia for a decade from 1979-89, with an administration led by Heng Samrin, a former Khmer Rouge, and Hun Sen, today's prime minister. Even though they rescued Cambodia from the genocidal regime, allowing international aid to be brought to the devastated country, many thousands of Cambodians fled to the borders of Thailand and filled the refugee camps.

It was here, safe at last, that a few surviving dancers started tentatively to go through the motions of an art that had almost perished with the majority of its practitioners.

Prince Norodom Sihamoni with the author.

[1]William Shawcross, *Sideshow*, 1979.

[2]Philip Short, *Pol Pot: The History of a Nightmare*, 2004.

[3]David Chandler, *Brother Number One*, 1999.

CHAPTER 8 SURVIVORS AND REBIRTH :
THE COSMIC AFTER THE CHAOTIC

Em Theay.

Buddhist monks on a peace march.

"I think the reason dance has held such an ageless magic for the world is that it has been the symbol of the performance of living. Even as I write, time has begun to make today yesterday – the past. ... But art is eternal, for it reveals the inner landscape, which is the soul of man," Martha Graham, *I Am A Dancer.*

Cambodian dance was kept alive in refugee camps such as Khao I Dang in Thailand by those who had escaped, and in towns in America and France to which Cambodians had fled as refugees. One of the surviving dancers was Mom Kamel who had been a star with Sihanouk's touring company in the 1950s, and Nuth Rachana, one of the first male palace dancers. Princess Buppha Devi visited the Thai refugee camps from France to give lessons. Meanwhile, survivors within the country, including performers and artists, started walking back to Phnom Penh, to find their colleagues and loved ones.

For those who were still alive, the same profound, visionary spirit that has driven artists from time immemorial to express ideas and to reach ever greater heights of achievement now propelled them towards rescuing their endangered art forms. Performing arts, more than individual art such as painting, have frequently been in the forefront of revival in the aftermath of destruction, as they are collective, involving groups of collaborators. Thus, dance, drama and music slowly came back into existence as performers worked together, assisting each other in the process of remembering – the word itself suggesting the remembering of what existed in their collective memories and had to be externalised before it was lost forever. Alongside these efforts, Buddhism in Cambodia was immediately revived, indicating the inextricable relationship of religion and society.

Survivors trained children and adults in the fragile tradition of master to disciple, encouraging them to learn the steps and dances that they were able to recall, hoping to pass them on to a new generation. This renaissance of the arts was more than the self expression of its individual practitioners; it was the rebirth of a culture, resonant with the spiritual and religious origins that were the foundation of Cambodia's – and most societies' – cultural values. It helped to re-establish what UNESCO, in defining culture, called "the set of distinctive spiritual, material, intellectual and emotional features of society or a social group" encompassing not only art, but "ways of living together, value systems, traditions and beliefs".

When, after World War II, Theodore Adorno, the German composer and philosopher, wrote his famous maxim, "Writing poetry after Auschwitz is barbaric" – inferring that the inspiration for poetry – and art – had been destroyed in the post-Holocaust era, the English poet Tony Harrison refuted his claim by writing: "There can *only* be poetry after Auschwitz."[1] Harrison, a distinctive voice of post-war experience, affirmed the ability of art to celebrate life even after the worst atrocities.

These artists were not only celebrating life and rebuilding their own systems of creative expression, they were contributing to the reconstruction of an entire society. There were 300 palace dancers before the Pol Pot regime, and only 30 came back. At first, survivors were afraid to return to the city and settled in areas just outside, in the suburbs, finding one another there. When they finally returned to Phnom Penh, it was to a deserted, annihilated city. With the heat and humidity of the tropical climate it had become overgrown with vegetation and weeds and was virtually uninhabitable. They lived in poverty, camping in derelict houses, or sleeping in the open, without electricity, water or sanitation, washing in the river each morning. A barter system existed in the absence of money.

They searched for fragments of costumes in the devastated national theatre where they found musical instruments filled with pigfood and masks thrown into gardens and paddy fields. They found pieces of old instruments such as abandoned drums among the rubbish that lay around the city.

A building was set aside for the artists to work in by Kev Chenda, a minister under the Vietnamese administration. Here, together, the dancers tried to piece together all the movements, reminding each other of details, trying to document the past. At best, the way in which dance is passed from generation to generation is fragile, a living art that is remembered from pupil to pupil. Those that had been killed took their memories with them, and the task that lay before the dancers seemed almost impossible. These 'old masters', overcoming their own personal suffering, dedicated themselves tirelessly to recreating the lost canon of dance and coaching new students. Never had the role of the *kru*, as 'master' and 'spirit', been more poignant. They became mentors, in the original sense of Mentor, the divine spirit who guides Telemachus in Homer's *Odyssey*.

With their help, a *corps de ballet* was reinstated and old dances started to come back to life. The first revival was the Wishing Dance, followed by the *Apsara* dance and *Moni Mekhala*. After the revival of *Tep Monorom* came the definite rebirth of classical dance.

With the 1993 United Nations-brokered democratic elections and re-crowning of Norodom Sihanouk came the start of peace. The coalition government that resulted, with Prince Norodom Ranariddh and Hun Sen as joint prime ministers, eventually gave way to the leadership of Hun Sen and, although it has not been without controversy, the country started gradually to rebuild its infrastructure. By 1994, the *Reamker* was sufficiently intact to be performed at a *Ramayana* festival and by 1997 about 50 percent of the classical ballet repertory had been rescued from extinction, notated, recorded in academic journals, photographed and videoed.

Among these heroic saviours of the performing arts were Chheng Phon, Pich Tum Kravel, Em Theay, Proeung Chhieng, Sam Satthya, Sophiline Cheam Shapiro, to name but a few of the Cambodians, and a number of committed foreigners who have brought their skills to the country.

Chheng Phon.

Chheng Phon

Emeritus Professor Chheng Phon, former head of the National Conservatory, director, dance researcher, musician, teacher and devout Buddhist, was a visionary and driving force during these post war years, finding artists and bringing them together when he became Minister of Culture. His career started as a young man when he had been a comic actor and dancer, performing as a clown, and was so fascinated by classical dance that he learned all the roles in the palace rehearsals, encouraged by the Queen Mother. He went on to become a professor at the University of Fine Arts as well as director of the National Conservatory. Among many other accomplishments, he preserved the fragile shadow puppet theatre of Cambodia during the early 1970s by establishing a performing arts farm for refugees and students at Obek Khaom, with performances of classical dance, *khol*, folk dance, *lakhon bassac*, and *yiké*.

During the savage years of the Pol Pot regime he miraculously managed to hide his identity and survived by looking after buffalo in Kompong Cham. "It was chance. It was luck. By some sort of magic I was saved. People in the villages who were not Polpotist saved me, I hid. I took off my glasses and had to feel my way around. I never said I could speak French. Before the war my wife and I had three children, and

A shadow puppet performance, Siem Reap. (PP)

Pich Tum Kravel.

13 orphans whom I looked after, I brought them up to be artists. During the Lon Nol regime I had an orphanage with more than 100 children. We lived in a house near Phnom Penh, at Stung Mentey, six kilometres away, which has long since gone, it was burned down." His three children are still alive. After the Pol Pot regime, he became Minister of Culture between 1981-1989. The Bassac Theatre became, once again, the focus of the intangible arts and the centre of the Department of Performing Arts, with a 268-strong company of dancers, musicians, acrobats and puppeteers. Now he has reinstated a Centre of Culture and Vipassana, a Buddhist ashram, in Takhmau, a suburb of Phnom Penh, creating a *theatre celeste*, with a grant of $300,000 from the city of Fukuoka in Japan. In conjunction with a United Nations High Commission for Refugees sponsored boat, he toured villages on the Mekong with performances. Surrounding himself with a collection of Cambodian silver pieces and Buddhist objects that were donated to him, and books ranging from Aeschyles to Musset, Corneille, Molière and Brecht, Chheng Phon has ensured that his three children have followed in his footsteps, all becoming involved in the arts.

Pich Tum Kravel

Professor Pich Tum Kravel, Under Secretary of State for the Performing Arts, Fine Arts and Libraries, a softly-spoken, grey-haired man, now in his late sixties, is an academic, writer, choreographer, former actor of stage and television and director of numerous productions of the *Reamker* as well as many contemporary plays. When we met, we spoke in French, an ability he had concealed during the Pol Pot regime for fear of being executed. We sat in his office at the back of the theatre, while he smoked cigarettes and drank tea, describing how he escaped the Khmer Rouge. In 1975 he managed to hide some of the puppets of the shadow theatre, and then escaped across the Mekong into the forests of Kompong Cham. In his book on shadow theatre[2], he writes poignantly about how the war pushed the Cambodian people "deeper and deeper into heartbreaking misery. Ears that used to relish sweet music heard only the sounds of guns and bombs. Eyes that used to delight in all kinds of plays saw only the savage, the tragic, the separation of loved ones, and the exodus from home villages. Noses used to elegant fragrances smelt only sour blood and gunpowder. The people lost their humanity. They like lived animals, like ghouls in a hell on earth."

When he returned to Phnom Penh in 1979 the theatre was in ruins, musical instruments had been destroyed, costumes torn to shreds and manuscripts burned. He worked feverishly with Chheng Phon to save as much as he could before it totally disappeared. One of the few writers and theatre directors to have stayed alive, he then wrote a modern play *The Life of the Nation of Kampuchea* which included scenes of Khmer Rouge brutality. It has played only a few times, and was first performed on 13 November, 1993, Independence Day, at the Bassac theatre, before it was damaged in a fire the following February. "I was directing it by day and still writing it at night," Pich Tum Kravel told me after I attended the opening night.

The play depicts the successive regimes of Sihanouk, Lon Nol and Pol Pot. In the dramatisation of the genocidal regime, Khmer Rouge soldiers burst on to the stage, shooting and beating people. They grabbed a woman's baby and dashed it against a wall. The woman began to wail and the audience laughed. It must have been a purging of emotions for them, a cathartic experience, the *mimesis* of Aristotle's theory of drama. Chhim Vatey, the actress who played the wailing woman, apparently wept during rehearsals. "It's difficult because it is so realistic, it touches everyone," admitted Kravel.

Kravel's courageous production of painful memories that affected both actors and audience are reminiscent of Augusto Boal's[3] approaches to the use of the dramatic process as a therapy for victims of oppression and torture. He uses theatre in the most archaic application of the word, the act of seeing, where all those involved, actors and spectators, are participants. Witnessing realistic scenes that conjure up memories for both enables them to see the actions differently, perhaps even laugh at them, and thus start the process of reconciliation needed to continue with their lives. This became the theme of Ong Keng Sen's *Continuum: Beyond the Killing Fields* (see below).

Those unimaginable horrors were experienced by Kravel's colleague, H E Professor Hang Soth, Director General of Techniques for Culture, Ministry of Culture and Fine Arts and Director of the National Theatre, who told me that of his and his wife's family, 27 members had died in the Pol Pot regime. He and Kravel, putting their own personal grief aside, have concentrated on rescuing the country's artistic past.

Adhering to the precious traditions of oral transmission of Khmer culture, Kravel found survivors and through them tried to reconstitute the masked theatre, shadow puppetry and dance using remnants of old recordings. In 1980 he helped Heng Samrin's Vietnamese government organise a national arts festival at the Bassac Theatre to determine how many artists were still alive. As they came forward, the School of Fine Arts was eventually able to reopen in 1981, enrolling 111 students to train in the traditional arts. The school was renamed the University of Fine Arts in 1988 and Royal University of Fine Arts when the monarchy was restored in 1993.

Today, 200 theatrical groups exist throughout the country, and Pich Tum Kravel has worked unceasingly to research the oral traditions of ethnic minorities and to record dances, music and poetry.

Proeung Chhieng

Proeung Chhieng, Vice Rector and Dean of Choreographic Arts at the Royal University of Fine Arts was born in 1949 and started dancing at the age of seven years old, specialising in the role of Hanuman, the monkey in the *Reamker*, because he loved acrobatics. His grandmother was a member of the royal dance troupe and he and his sister, also a royal dancer, watched her in the palace grounds while she trained. At the age of eight, he started formal training under her tutelage and at 17 began to teach. His first salary was only 25 *riels*, but after graduating to principal dancer with the Royal Cambodian Ballet, he received a scholarship to go to North Korea. He returned in 1975, just as the Khmer Rouge seized power. In all innocence he was going to tell them that he was a dancer, but was warned not to and to pretend he could not read or write. Hiding his identity saved his life. He was forced into the countryside, labouring in the ricefields, suffering starvation and deprivation. In 1979, he returned to Phnom Penh, found other survivors and helped to reconstruct the repertory of dance. He says

that although some of the dances have been recreated, others have been only partly restored, as steps and movements have been irretrievably forgotten. He helped to re-establish the Royal University of Fine Arts, and forged links to refugee communities in Thailand, the USA and Europe, and has been a dedicated supporter of Princess Buppa Devi. "Dance is our national soul," he says.

Proeung Chhieng is dedicated to publicising the importance of Cambodian dance. During the last two decades he has organised numerous dance tours throughout the world, invited scholars from abroad to teach and research, and has represented Cambodia at international conferences and workshops. He is co-director of the Cambodian Arts Mentorship Program, a teaching and documentation program administered by the Asian Cultural Council, a senior consultant to the Japan Foundation-funded Dance Notation Project, and an advisor to Cambodia's minister of culture. In recognition of his important contribution to the study, understanding and practice of performing arts, he received the John D. Rockefeller 3rd Award from the Asian Cultural Council.

"The role of all artists in the world is to teach people to love good rather than evil," he told me. "We are peace messengers. We dance to ask the gods to help our country. People are born and die. But the country never dies. My art is my life. I want to preserve our culture. This is not only for Cambodia, but for the world, like the temples of Angkor Wat."

Em Theay

Em Theay is a radiant silver haired woman who is always smiling, a figure of exceptional dignity, serenity and grace, enhanced by her advancing years. She bears no hatred or desire for revenge for what she endured but, on the contrary, possesses a sense of acceptance and magnanimity that is inspiring. When I asked her how she lives with the memory of the Pol Pot regime, she said: "I don't think about the past, I focus on now, on gathering together the classical dances. I am too old, I want to make the most of the time now."

Proeung Chhieng.

Em Theay teaching.

Em Theay with daughter Preab, left, and Sotho Kulikar, right.

Kim Bun Thom.

Star of an emotional television documentary *The Tenth Dancer* by Australian director Sally Ingleton, released in 1993, Em Theay is among the ten percent of palace dancers who survived. Her mother worked in the palace as a cook and, as a child, Em Theay followed her around, watching the palace dancers rehearsing and imitating them. One day, when she was just seven years old, Queen Kossamak heard her singing in the garden, and realised she had potential to be a singer and dancer. Em Theay went on to train, dancing and singing and performing the Ogre, or Demon, role. At the height of her career, she danced for President Richard Nixon in America. She married a palace soldier in her late teens, and gave birth 18 times, although some of her children died in infancy through natural causes – in Cambodia, the infant mortality rate is high. Nevertheless, she has always been dedicated to dance.

She lost her husband, five of her children and her three sisters in the Pol Pot regime, as well as countless friends and colleagues. She was in the palace when the Khmer Rouge invaded. From there she rushed to her home, but her children had already gone. She was forced to march out of the city, managing to conceal her identity. Somehow she was not killed, and managed to secrete away in a bag the dance book and song book given to her by the Queen, her sole possessions after the mass evacuation. She was forced to go first to Kandal province, then later to Battambang. "My children were sent to another place," she recalled. "Under the Khmer Rouge we were not allowed to live together. I was forced to work in the rice fields." She recounts how Khmer Rouge soldiers made her dance for them, jeering at her. But this was, miraculously, what saved her. Her village chief liked her singing and decided that she should sing the babies to sleep rather than continue her arduous physical labour on the land.

One day she learned about the death of one of her children. "I asked *Angkar* (the ruling authority) if I could go and see him, but they wouldn't let me go." Then she heard that two more of her children had died. Overcome with grief, she became ill, but was forced to continue working until she collapsed. She was sent to a hospital but while she was there discovered that she was going to be killed. Again, by chance, she was saved, but was by now too ill to work and was assigned to look after the children of the community where she sang songs to them. When another of her sons died, she was afraid to show her grief in case she

would be killed too. They would not allow her to see his body and she does not know where he is buried.

She says she lost 300 artist friends and colleagues during the Khmer Rouge regime. She is one of the few fortunate artists who survived. In the *The Tenth Dancer*, Em Theay and her pupil, the dancer Sok Chay, describe their lives during this period and the horror is evoked intercutting their memories with archive footage of Pol Pot.

In 1979 she was in Battambang when she heard that Pol Pot had fled after the Vietnamese invasion. "We started our escape, without shoes. Along the way we witnessed battles between Khmer Rouge and Vietnamese soldiers. I remember a bombed out pagoda. Everything was completely destroyed, only the Buddha was still standing. We stopped at Battambang to search for our loved ones who had escaped from other labour camps. I met an old student who invited me to teach dance at a school which had just opened a month ago. After a few days, I forced my family to continue to Phnom Penh. It took a month to walk back, 170 miles. Wherever I stopped I taught dance."

In Phnom Penh the Ministry of Culture found out that she was still alive and asked her to come back to teach. "At first we got paid with a rice allowance," she remembered. Her five surviving children are all dancers.

Her daughter Kim Ann Thong, whose nickname is Preab, who has seven children, is a dancer and travels with her on tours. Em Theay has 11 grandchildren, and two more emerged when she visited London on tour in 2005. An article in *The Times* had mentioned that on a previous visit, her son had stayed behind, married another Cambodian dancer, and fathered twins, but then died. The twins were reunited with their grandmother after the performance at the Institute of Contemporary Arts in London.

"Today I am retired but I still teach classical dances and songs at Royal University of Fine Arts to the new generations. I love my art and I would do everything, anything for the life of my performing art."

Kim Ann Thong (Preab)

Em Theay's daughter Preab lost one child and her husband. She remembered how she had to leave Phnom Penh during the mass evacuations with her four-year-old boy and one-year-old girl. She was eight months pregnant. On the way to the labour camp in

Battambang she gave birth to her third child, a son. Her daughter soon died of fever, an event she can never forget, as she felt responsible for her death, having chased her away from the cornfields while Khmer Rouge soldiers threatened her for stopping work.

Her husband was arrested and executed in 1976 as a result of her pleading with the village chief not to separate them, a tragic scene that she relived during each performance of Ong Keng Sen's moving production *The Continuum: Beyond The Killing Fields*. She again felt responsible for his death. She remarried, and confesses in the play that she did so only in order to have children. When I interviewed her she said: "I only think about now, for my children, all seven of them, are dancers, musicians and painters."

Kim Bun Thom

A gentle dancer with an expressive face, she was on the verge of being forced to marry a legless soldier during the Pol Pot regime. (Cambodia was one of the most heavily landmined countries in the world with an estimated 10 million after the war, although the temple and tourist areas have all been cleared now). Distraught and crying, she was saved by a stranger who intervened and offered to marry her instead. This was how she met her husband. But when she became pregnant, she was so frightened about the future of her child in such a gruelling society, that her husband helped her to abort with traditional medicine. Of her extended family of 40, including aunts and uncles and cousins, only four returned from the labour camps. Telling her story in a dramatic context of *The Continuum*, including her husband's infidelity and their subsequent divorce has, she said, helped her "build a better sense of peace within myself."

Chea Samy

The late Chea Samy, whose health was broken by years of starvation and hard labour, was still teaching dancing on my first visit to the School of Fine Arts in 1993. She found it hard to stand and walk as her knees were so weak. A farmer's daughter, at the age of five years old she longed to be a dancer after seeing a folk dance troupe perform in her village. She auditioned for the dance school at the royal palace when she was six, in 1925, and, in spite of competition from thousands of children, was awarded a place. She danced the clas-

sical roles, playing both male and female parts, as was the tradition. She was a living repository of history, having met King Sisowath and Princess Soumphady, danced for King Monivong, of whom she was a mistress, and performed for King Norodom Sihanouk.

She had no idea that Saloth Sar was Pol Pot until much later during the regime. Having hidden her own identity to save her life, she was working in a communal kitchen washing dishes for 700 people when she saw a photograph of Pol Pot and instantly recognised her little brother-in-law.

She returned to Phnom Penh with another survivor, Keo Malis, in 1980 to try to find other friends and colleagues. Her house had been torn down and used for firewood by the Khmer Rouge. Chea Samy taught until she died in June 1994.

Sam Sathya

The beautiful ballet star Sam Sathya was just six years old when the Khmer Rouge invaded in 1975, filling her with fear, terror and incomprehension. When she finally returned to Phnom Penh, having walked 300 kilometres barefoot, she learned to treasure simple pleasures again, cherishing family life and being able to go to school. She went to a dance rehearsal one day and met Chheng Phon and was soon taking lessons with Chea Samy and Proeung Chhieng. Although she found the lessons difficult and painful, she persevered, and graduated in 1989, one of the first graduates of the School of Fine Arts. Her classic beauty and poise made her a perfect choice for the role of Seda in the *Reamker*.

Sotho Kulikar

Kulikar was born in 1975 and never knew her father who was killed during the Pol Pot regime. She has studied dance for seven years. "The future of dance in Cambodia is now booming, everyone is interested in dance, more and more children are coming to classes," she said. She performs and teaches, and appeared in *The Continuum*. But she is also working as a businesswoman and raising a family.

Sam Sathya.

Chea Samy in 1994 teaching.

Soth Somaly.

Mann Kosal

A charismatic and virile dancer, Mann Kosal, who also appeared in *The Continuum*, is now a leading shadow puppeteer with a theatrical organisation in Phnom Penh called Souvanna Phum. One of 12 children, Mann Kosal spent much of the Khmer Rouge years on the run, hiding in forests and scavenging for food for his ailing mother. In *The Continuum* he describes his gnarling hunger during the Pol Pot regime and the chilling fear that gripped him when his workmates in the labour camp were murdered in front of him.

"We can't forget what happened," he said, "but now we want our lives back."

He trained at the Royal University of Fine Arts and started making large leather shadow puppets, *sbek thom*, virtually creating a life for himself with his bare hands (see Chapter 11).

Soth Somaly

Soth Somaly, who was born in 1957, has danced since the age of five years old. She is a teacher, choreographer and costume designer at the Royal University of Fine Arts. Her grandmother and mother were dance teachers, and now her daughter is teaching dance too.

"I was there at the mass exodus from Phnom Penh," she said. "I was 15 years old. Pol Pot's soldiers stopped my parents from coming with me, and I left with my aunt." A pupil of Chea Samy, she concealed her dance background and was forced to do hard labour in the fields. At night she dreamed of dance and when she couldn't sleep would try to remember all the steps and sequences. During the regime she lost her sister, brother-in-law, neice and nephew. On her return to the city in 1980 she began teaching, and now gives classical dance lessons to 160 students, 130 of whom are girls. "I started to teach in Kompong Thom and then the Culture Minister Chheng Phon invited me to come here in 1987." She also teaches folkloric dance and shadow play.

She sighs when I mention the newly built campus for the Royal University of Fine Arts in Russei Keo, nine kilometres northwest of Phnom Penh, difficult to reach for many of the students and staff. She says that some of the teachers cannot get there as they do not have the money for petrol. Their salary is just $30 per month. Although money is needed for everything from costumes to paper, she nevertheless believes that the outlook for the future is good.

Sophiline Cheam Shapire.

Sophiline Cheam Shapiro

Sophiline was among the first dancers to graduate from the University of Fine Arts when it re-opened in the 1980s. During the Khmer Rouge period Sophiline was just a child, but her work is a celebration of the revival of dance after the devastation, and a contribution to its evolution as she brings new creativity to a classical art form. She was born in 1967 in Phnom Penh. Her childhood ended abruptly in 1975 when the Khmer Rouge invaded the city, marching everyone into the countryside. She lost her father, two brothers, her grandmother, uncles and cousins. "We lost everything," she said. "I am no different from most of my generation. I know of almost no family that survived without losses." In *Children of Cambodia's Killing Fields: Memoirs by Survivors*, compiled by Dith Pran, she describes how she was forced to sing Khmer Rouge songs that, paradoxically, helped her to survive.

After the Vietnamese invasion of 1979 and the disappearance of Pol Pot, people gradually returned to the

deserted capital, and Sophiline found herself with her uncle, Chheng Phon. As he gathered together the surviving performers, one night after dinner she started to sing. When Chheng Phon heard her, he persuaded her to join the theatre school. He warned her that to be a dancer was short-lived but that acting could continue indefinitely. "But my voice changed," she recalled, "so I went into dancing after all." When the School of Fine Arts reopened in 1981, it enrolled 111 students, of whom Sophiline was one.

She was taught by the surviving inheritors of the ancient court traditions. Her teachers, Soth Samon, now 75, and Chea Samy, who died in 1994, suggested she learn the Giant and other male roles of dance drama, always played by women, in keeping with the practice of perfecting just one role in the repertoire. But her delicate physical stature limited her abilities and she turned to female roles. She graduated in 1988, with the first post-war generation of performers, and became a Faculty member. With the University of

Mann Kosal making a shadow puppet.

Fine Arts company, now the Royal University, she toured abroad in Vietnam, India, the Soviet Union and the USA.

Sophiline has adapted Khmer classical ballet to other theatrical forms and her latest creation, *Pamina Devi*, a Cambodian version of Mozart's *Magic Flute*, was shown in Vienna in December 2006. A collaboration with Amrita Performing Arts, it was commissioned by American director Peter Sellars as part of the New Crowned Hope Festival designed to commemorate the 250th anniversary of Mozart's birth and to pose the question of how Mozart would have composed today.

She adapted this classic art form so that it has become enriched by new influences, a development that has not always met with approval from her Cambodian counterparts. Taking the story of the *Magic Flute* she has transformed Pamina, Queen of the Night, into a Cambodian dancer, Devi. The many ideas running through Mozart's work echo numerous strands within the *Reamker*. Its recurring theme is the triumph of good over evil. Pamina Devi, a beautiful and mysterious seductress, is a dangerous yet fascinating power, representing the irrational and the diabolic. Her nature contrasts with that of her antagonist, Sarastro, who symbolises a reasonable sovereign with paternalistic wisdom, and his enlightened insight ultimately enables him to overcome her. While the love story between Pamina and Tamino touches a universal chord, Mozart's enigmatic work, filled with symbols, resonates at many levels within a Cambodian artistic framework that Sophiline has managed to explore.

She has also choreographed other ballets. *Samritechak*, a dance interpretation of Shakespeare's *Othello*, was created in 2000 and performed at the Venice Biennale, the Hong Kong Festival and America's Long Beach Carpenter Center. *The Glass Box* was shown in Los Angeles in 2002 and Cambodia and India in 2003, while *Seasons of Migration*, a story of culture shock, was danced by the Royal University of Fine Arts ensemble at its premiere in Long Beach in April 2005.

While on tour in America in 1991 she met and married writer John Shapiro. She moved to California, later giving birth to twin sons, Cameron and Eli. In Long Beach she began teaching dance in the refugee Cambodian community there, the largest in America, with some 40,000 people. She studied dance ethnology at the University of California and taught classical

Mann Kosal at Angkor Wat. Still from *The Continuum*. Photograph Chris Kutschera.

Left: **Sophiline Cheam Shapiro on right, choreographing Pamina Devi.**

Samritechak. The role of Iago is played as a monkey.

Samritechak.

dance in the World Arts & Cultures Department. She started her own company, *Danse Celeste*, and co-founded the Khmer Arts Academy, a performing arts organisation of which she is Artistic Director. Dedicated to Cambodian arts, it has a resident ensemble that performs regionally and on tour. She has received numerous awards, including a Guggenheim Fellowship, a Durfee Foundation Master Musician Fellowship, an Irvine Fellowship in Dance and in 2007 was the youngest ever winner of the prestigious Nikkei Asia Prize.

With the $30,000 Irvine Fellowship she embarked on the creation of *Samritechak* in 1998. Her aim was to build a cultural bridge between her two worlds by taking a classic Western drama and interpreting it through ancient Cambodian dance and song, challenging new artistic understanding about the nature of theatre and tragedy.

Drawing on Shakespeare's tale of the Moor of Venice, his jealousy and betrayal, she drew parallels between the innocence of Desdemona and that of Seda (Sita), the heroine of the *Reamker*. Shakespeare's plays were acted entirely by men, with boys playing the female parts, while Cambodian dance is performed by women, including the male roles. In Sophiline's pro-

duction, accompanied by a sung chorus, her stroke of originality was to have Iago portrayed as a monkey, making reference not only to one of the protagonists of the *Reamker*, Hanuman, but also illuminating facets of Shakespeare's meddling, voluble character. *Othello*, preoccupied as it is with the tension between harmony and chaos, has particular relevance in Cambodia, and the fact that Iago's evil is beyond comprehension mirrors Cambodia's recent history which defies explanation. While Cambodian dance is about mythological characters rather than real people, the central theme is always the triumph of good over evil, thus reflecting fundamental aspects of Shakespeare's play. But the final scene of *Othello* taking his own life through guilt, acting as his own judge, is a contrast to the reality of Cambodia, where unrepentant murderers of the Pol Pot regime are still at large. Sophiline says her aim was to show that ultimately people have to take responsibility for their actions.

Seasons of Migration was another reinterpretation of Cambodian mythology, interwoven with her own personal artistic journey, which was tinged with guilt at having left Cambodia for America. Influenced by two different cultures, and feeling dislocated, Sophiline fused the stylised forms of Cambodian dance with

dynamic movements from Western choreographers such as George Balanchine and Merce Cunningham. The piece focuses on a *naga*, the multi-headed serpent of Hindu mythology and progenitor of the Khmer race, depicted as coiled in its own tail, turning and twisting to free itself. Symbolically, it alludes to Sophiline's own experiences, the joy of being in a new world, followed by confusion and loss of identity. It progresses through disintegration to reintegration, concluding with harmony between past and present.

The production was greeted with reservations by Cambodians, in particular Proeung Chhieng, Dean of Choreography at the Royal University of Fine Arts, but after seeing it again, he told journalist Seth Mydans in an inteview that it pointed to the future of Cambodian dance. Sophiline adds that to increase the repertory of dance will help to preserve it and prevent it from atrophying or becoming a museum piece. "I have always been committed to preserving classic Cambodian dance," she emphasised. "My ancestors created something unique to history. I only have the privilege to try to make it better. I think I would be a criminal if I did anything to destroy it."

Sophine is taking dance to new heights, putting it on the international stage. Her productions introduce audiences to the ancient court dance of Cambodia while redefining the role of dance and its future within the country today.

Opposite bottom right and below: **Pamina Devi choreographed by Sophiline Cheam Shapiro**.

Rithy Panh with the author.
Photo: Martin Flitman.

Rithy Panh was hailed as an extraordinary talent after his film *The People of the Ricefields* was nominated for the Palme d'Or at the Cannes Film Festival in 1994. This eloquent film shows the lives of a peasant family tending their rice fields. With simplicity and subtlety the story illustrates the harshness of their existence while lingering on the beauty of the countryside and the dignity of the people. Only one fleeting scene alludes to the memory of the Khmer Rouge and the effect on their lives. "The role of the artist," he claims, "is to awaken peoples' consciousness, show them a sensitivity, a tradition, a history, a culture. When there are difficulties, the force of a country is in its soul. Its soul is its culture. The artist can speak to poor people and make them rich, by giving them back their dignity. When the world is ugly, then you show the beauty, the sincerity."

Catherine Geach

In 1993 an English violinist, Catherine Geach, then only 18 years old, started teaching violin at the Royal University of Fine Arts. She went on to set up a Khmer classical music school in Kampot for orphaned and handicapped children. It was successful enough that by 1997 she was able to arrange a tour for them to play in Europe. The Music School is part of the Khmer Cultural Development Institute, a Cambodian non-governmental organisation. It aims to promote the preservation and re-establishment of traditional musical culture.

Geach has specialised in teaching children who have been orphaned or who are traumatised, abused or handicapped. Alongside those who have been severely wounded and mutilated by some of the millions of landmines still hidden in the fields, there are many children who have been deformed for life by untreated illnesses such as polio. Music and dance can help these damaged children.

William Lobban

Lobban, an ethnomusicologist from Adelaide, worked for six years in Cambodia as a volunteer Visiting Professor at RUFA, helping to revive music and dance as well as assisting with redesigning classical costumes.

He arrived in 1987 on an organised tour of Angkor and instantly "fell in love with the place" and decided

Rithy Panh

A young cineaste in his 40s, Rithy Panh has recently made a recent film about the burned out Bassac theatre and the plight of the performers, called *Les Artistes du Théatre Brulée*. Cinema became the artistic medium for Rithy following a ten year silence after the Pol Pot regime.

Born in 1964, he suffered the horrors of the Khmer Rouge in a re-education camp. He escaped across minefields to the Thai border in 1979. Thirteen members of his family, including his parents and three of his eight brothers and sisters died. From there he fled to France where he cut himself off from his culture. "I wanted to forget what happened," he said. "I wanted to be alone. For ten years I had no contact with anything Cambodian. I was writing poetry, playing music, painting, solitary activities." He then went into cinema, and returned to Cambodia in 1990. Since then he has been making films and teaching younger students, using cinema to resurrect the culture of his country.

He brought together a group of actors from the Preah Suramarit Theatre (the Bassac Theatre), filming them on a daily basis in this desolate, burned ruin, evoking memories of a time when they performed each evening, and reflecting the way in which the country has evolved since the genocide. Today, when there are so few cinemas and theatre, it is a poignant story.

Ethnomusicologist Bill Lobban looks on as a Fine Arts School instrument maker heats up metal drills for fabricating parts in the School workshop. Photo H Smith, Courtesy Australian War Memorial. (Negative No. PO3258.344)

to work as a volunteer. He started to teach music at the Royal University of Fine Arts. Financial restrictions made it difficult to buy the necessary materials as the classical music section of the University had no funding. For example, to tune their musical instruments, the students needed lead and beeswax, which the they could not afford to buy. Lobban bought it for them and for the first time in seven years students were able to tune their instruments.

Most musical instruments had been destroyed during the Pol Pot regime, used as cooking pots or left outside to perish in the rain. Writing about his research in 1990[4], Lobban stated that of the two heavily inlaid and ornamented orchestras that were part of the former royal palace music ensemble, only two instruments were ever recovered, in 1979. One was too badly damaged to use. He adds that there were just 47 musicians and dancers left from the former National Theater and Fine Arts School to help teach at the new Fine Arts School.

During his research he realised that most of the instruments of a classical orchestra could be made with indigenous materials. For example, flutes of various sizes could be constructed from bamboo and reeds that grow in swamps and marshes, while wind instruments could be made from buffalo horn. Finding rosewood for the cases and the keys of the *roneat*, a xylophone, from the area of the Elephant Mountains

and forests of Kratie was still problematic during the 1990s as there were attacks from the Khmer Rouge in the area.

With support from Save the Children Fund Australia and Australian Volunteers Abroad, Lobban helped the Fine Arts School construct a workshop in 1988 for making instruments, purchase supplies and train young craftspeople. Extra instruments could be sold to provide cash for the workshop. In 1989 the International Catholic Relief funded the building of a forge next to the instruments workshop. These two buildings gave the school space for making traditional instruments, and training a new generation of craftspeople.

As a musicologist Lobban was acutely aware of the fleeting nature of memory and anxious to capture every possible musical recollection. In particular, he encouraged Em Theay, who had a good memory, to recall her repertoire of songs from her years at the palace before the Pol Pot regime. He bought her a tape recorder so that whenever she remembered a fragment, she would immediately record it. There are now 1,700 songs registered.

Lobban was fascinated by classical dance and to help the dancers and teachers study the movements as they remembered them, he took more than 8,000 photographs. Each would reveal the nuances of gestures and steps. To help recreate the glittering costumes, for

Fred Frumberg with Proeung Chhieng.

which the materials in Cambodia were nonexistent and the few garments that existed were worn over and over again, he even brought back nine kilos of sequins from Australia, an event he described to me with much amusement as he recalled bringing them through customs.

Lobban accompanied the dancers on one of their earliest foreign tours, to Britain, in 1989, where they performed in Glasgow and Oxford.

Fred Frumberg

Fred Frumberg, an American who arrived in Cambodia in 1997 as a United Nations volunteer, has raised money and awareness for dance performances nationally and internationally. In 2003, with support from the Rockefeller Foundation, he set up a performing arts non-government organisation (NGO) called Amrita – Sanskrit for eternity – its name reinforcing the belief in the 'eternity' of the performing arts. Frumberg came to Cambodia with a wealth of experience of the performing arts after a career that included working as opera stage manager in San Francisco and at the Komische Oper in former East Berlin, followed by a seven-year collaboration with Peter Sellars as assistant director and producer on opera, theater and video projects throughout Europe and the USA, and culminating as Head of the Stage Directing Department at the Paris National Opera. He came to help in the revival and preservation of Cambodia's performing arts, in collaboration with UNESCO and the Cambodian Ministry of Culture and Fine Arts.

Reviving classics, he has also developed cross-cultural projects with regional partners in Southeast Asia and the US. With his support, productions have toured the US, Australia, France, Italy, India and Singapore. For example, he brought a production to the Singapore Art Festival in 2007 directed by Annemarie Prins entitled simply *Three years, eight months and 20 days*, the duration of the Pol Pot regime. It was a dramatised recollection by three women who lived through it, losing their loved ones. Frumberg believes in the use of the performing arts as a vehicle for bringing historic events back into the public consciousness. He was also concerned that the Pol Pot regime was not taught in

Arn Chorn-Pond in *The Flute Player*.

schools in Cambodia until recently so that children knew about the genocide only from their parents. Reaction to this play has revealed how much Cambodians want to recall their experiences in order to find a resolution. Similar in its ethos and impact to the work of Pich Tum Kravel and Ong Keng Sen, this piece is another example of the use of theatre, of mimesis and catharsis, where there is a therapeutic effect.

Arn Chorn-Pond, John Burt, Charley Todd

Two Americans, John Burt and Charley Todd, became Chair of the Board and Co-President respectively of a non-government organisation called Cambodian Living Arts. It was founded in 1998 by Arn Chorn-Pond, a Cambodian musician whose flute playing saved his life during the Pol Pot regime, the subject of a PBS documentary *The Flute Player* in 2003. From his extended family of 40 members, only two of his sisters survived the slaughter. Adopted by American parents, Arn Chorn-Pond became a human rights speaker and activist for Amnesty International, co-founded Children of War in America and was founder of the Cambodian Master Performers Programme.

When Arn Chorn-Pond and John Burt met they found that they shared many interests as Burt, a theatre director, had been leading a national tour of youths telling stories about life in the nuclear age, while Chorn-Pond had been working on a comparable project about children's wartime experiences.

With Burt as executive producer, they have directed a new production, *Where Elephants Weep*, the first contemporary Cambodian opera, loosely inspired by Chorn-Pond's life. It explores the experiences of Cambodians such as Chorn-Pond returning to their homeland to discover their cultural heritage and roots. A blend of Eastern traditional music and Western rocks songs, it opened in 2007 in America, in Lowell, home to the second largest Cambodian population in the country, after California.

Burt and Chorn-Pond have sought out surviving musicians in Cambodia and now teach 500 students to play traditional instruments. They have also focused on the many disabled people in Cambodia. Victims of landmines or the ravages of polio – there are some 45,000 amputees in the country – whose lives have been transformed by charities such as the Cambodia

Trust which makes prosthetic limbs, also have an artistic contribution to make. Cambodian Living Arts has helped to train and support hundreds of disabled performing artists as well as children from impoverished backgrounds, organising music, dance and opera performances for them. Their mission is to the support the revival of traditional art forms in Cambodia and to inspire contemporary artistic expression. They are looking ahead to 2020 when, they hope, Cambodia will experience a cultural renaissance so dynamic that the arts will have become the country's international signature. They believe Khmer arts "will become a wellspring of strength and resilience, and a vital source for healing and reconciliation."

In particular, they have worked with a group of about 100 performers who were squatting in a derelict development, apartments that were built during the Sihanouk years, known now as Tonle Bassac, close to the Bassac theatre, earmarked for demolition at the time of writing. Their work here has been inspirational as many of the performers are children who, without this help, would have had no opportunity to become artists, dancers, singers and musicians.

Ong Keng Sen

The work of Singaporean Ong Keng Sen, a former law student, now avant-garde director of Singapore's TheatreWorks, blended new and ancient theatrical forms when he created a drama in Cambodia that had the killing fields as its theme. *Continuum: Beyond the Killing Fields* is a tour de force. It has been performed internationally, including in London in 2005. This daring and dramatic piece of theatre, with video, live performance and music, reflecting Pich Tum Kravel's earlier ideas of drama therapy, is powerful in its emotions and shocking in its revelations of the suffering experienced by three classical dancers and a shadow puppeteer who survived forced labour camps in Battambang province during the Pol Pot regime. Ong Keng Sen is an exciting, innovative director, using material in a challenging way, mixing artists from different backgrounds together in freely experimental ways that he calls "cultural negotiation." He knew he was uncovering grief, yet at the same time, through performance, achieving a healing. Inspired by Japanese Noh Theatre, he gives the audience the script to read, translated from Khmer into English, as the performance progresses so

that they can appreciate the different language, the atmosphere it creates and the emotions it produces.

The piece starts with a video clip of the dancers in Phnom Penh, prior to departure, making spiritual offerings to their teachers, their gurus. Then the live drama opens with an empty stage and three spotlights under which three dancers in traditional costumes, Preab, Em Theay and Kulikar, are seated on the ground. The use of shadow puppetry is exceptionally striking, with the lone male actor, Mann Kosal, leaping behind and in front of a backlit screen. A film sequence shows the making of the puppets, starting with the leather drying. Then the dancers tell their poignant stories in segments, interspersed with dance sequences, accompanied only by singing.

Each remembers the horrors, the killings, the persecutions, the loss. Preab, for example, describes the traumatic departure from Phnom Penh with her children and the death of her daughter and husband. Em Theay, lit by a single spotlight, recalls her years of forced labour in the fields and the deaths of her children. Kulikar recounts how Neak Kru (Master) Em Theay learned to dance when she was seven years old. She was chosen by the Queen Kossamak to dance the classical demon role. Kulikar says that Em Theay lost 300 artist friends during the Khmer Rouge regime. She is one of the few fortunate artists who survived. Today she is perhaps the only living archive of Cambodian classical dances songs. "Why would our own people want to kill us?" laments Kulikar.

Ong Keng Sen.

A still from *The Continuum: Beyond the Killing Fields*. **Photograph Chris Kutschera**.

Their memories are so distressing that they weep on stage. The sound effects such as a whistling wind herald the stories. Towards the end, as the horrors recede, with the stories told, the stage is then black. But the audience then becomes aware of a faintly shimmering presence. A soft light grows imperceptibly stronger gradually illuminating an increasingly glittering figure until the full costume of the dancer appears like a vision, bathed in golden light, as if the sun has risen. She then starts, slowly, to dance a sequence, the triumph of revival after the terror of destruction.

Dramatising these terrible memories in a poignant style, Ong Keng Sen mixed personal narratives with classical dance and scenes from the *Reamker*, as well as shadow puppetry. Just as in Pich Tum Kravel's *The Life of the Nation of Kampuchea* with its episodes of Khmer Rouge brutality, there is a cathartic purging of emotions in *Continuum* for actors and spectators, who undergo the mimesis of Aristotle's theory of drama.

Continuum is timely in its efforts to heal the traumas as only now has the government embarked on United Nations-sponsored court hearings for the genocide in Cambodia. Khieu Sampan, Ieng Sary and Nuon Chea have been detained for trials, but are elderly and infirm. However, justice will at last be seen to be done so that this brutal chapter of Cambodia's history can be consigned to the past.

In November 2004, King Sihanouk, also ailing, gave up his throne and Norodom Sihamoni, former choreographer and dancer, was crowned king.

UNESCO

On 7 November 2003 Koïchiro Matsuura, Director General of UNESCO, proclaimed the Royal Ballet of Cambodia to be a masterpiece of oral and intangible heritage. Following the inscription of the Historic Site of Angkor as a World Heritage Site, Khmer classical dance is now also part of the heritage of humanity.

This event is a milestone in the action to safeguard and promote Khmer classical dance and Cambodian intangible heritage. This international distinction honours the most remarkable examples of oral traditions and forms of cultural expression in all regions of the world. Through this definitive and prompt action, the programme underlines the importance of safeguarding and protecting oral and intangible heritage.

The Ministry of Culture and Fine Arts plans to submit other applications, including one for masked theatre, *lakhon khol*, big shadow puppet or *sbaek thom*, the work of the silversmiths, *cheang prak*, Khmer traditional silk and the traditional story tellers *chapei*.

Thanks to all of these people, the sacred dance has been preserved not only for Cambodia but for the world.

[1] Tony Harrison, *Prometheus*, 1998.

[2] Pich Tum Kravel, Slok Thom (Khmer Shadow Theatre), 1995.

[3] Auguste Boel, *Theatre of the Oppressed*, 1979.

[4] William Lobban, *Making the Traditional Musical Instruments of Cambodia*, 1990.

Em Theay in *The Continuum: Beyond the Killing Fields*.
Photograph Chris Kutschera.

Murals illustrating the *Reamker* in the Royal Palace.

"The stage … is a temple where the religion of a poetical interpretation and symbolical celebration of life is communicated." Eugene O'Neill.

To watch a theatrical performance involves a "willing suspension of disbelief," as Coleridge described it, to enter a world of the imagination in which the spectator will temporarily believe. In Cambodian dance the stage takes on a symbolic aspect, representing the terrestrial world where the performance is an invocation to the celestial realm. As dance evolved from a ritual within the temple to a dramatisation within the court, its sanctity remained, for dancers embodied the spirits and the distinction between sacred and secular was non-existent.

The subject matter of dance

In Cambodia, dance came to have two functions. There were the ancient rituals and ceremonies, *robam*, the generic Khmer word for dance, and the later dramatisation of stories, *roeung*, including the epics. While the latter were performed in conjunction with ceremonies and always preceded by a sacred offering, they were not in themselves ritual performances.

Audiences, suspending their disbelief, participate in the mystical realm of the religious epics and in Cambodian dance the subject matter and visual content are invariably fantastical. Sanskrit inscriptions at early Angkorian temples allude to recitations of the *Mahabharata* and *Ramayana* as a way of gaining merit, suggesting that performance was a sacred activity. But it was predominantly the *Ramayana*, reinterpreted as the *Reamker*, that was chosen as the dramatic vehicle in Cambodia. It had a powerful hold on the Khmer imagination and superceded the *Mahabharata* following the rise of Buddhism and adoption of Pali canonical texts instead of Sanskrit literature. Productions of the *Mahabharata* are still popular in India, however, and have even been televised so that the younger generation will be familiar with the multitude of characters and stories. Scenes from both epics are depicted at the temples of Angkor.

The *Ramayana* and the *Mahabharata* were conceived in classical Sanskrit in India in about 400 BC. The *Mahabharata*, which appears in earlier carved narrative bas reliefs at Angkor[1] is the longest poem in the world. It is composed of 90,000 verses, *slokas*, formalised into a compendium of tales, myths and legends, the most comprehensive document for ancient Indian life and its religious, ethical and social traditions. At its heart is the epic struggle between two dynastic families, the Pandavas and the Kauravas, that reaches a climactic confrontation at the Battle of Kurukshetra which lasts 18 days. This is preceded by the *Bhagavad Gita*, the 'Song of the Lord', Prince Arjuna's spiritual dialogue with Krishna, his mentor and charioteer, before he goes into battle. These 700 verses of sublime instruction are the most influential of Hindu

Murals *Reamker*, Royal Palace.

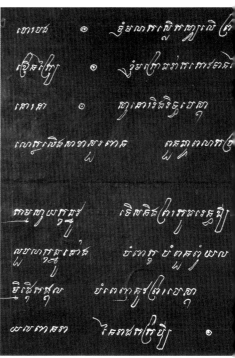

Part of a *Reamker* manuscript in the British Library. The paper made from tree bark was folded accordion-like into a book. It was then frequently blackened with starch and charcoal with yellow ink for the writing.

scriptures and were recited daily by figures such as Mahatma Gandhi.

Both narrative poems were originally handed down through the oral tradition, but the *Ramayana*, meaning The Glory of Rama, narrated by the poet and sage Valmiki, is the older of the two. It describes the exploits of Prince Rama, the seventh earthly incarnation of the god Vishnu from whom he has inherited perfection and kindness, and his quest to rescue his beloved wife Sita from a demon king. Before Rama's birth, the gods determined his life would be one of a hero who would be tested. The 48,000 line odyssey, comprising 24,000 verses, divided into seven principal cantos, *kandas*, is a moral tale about the triumph of good over evil, of heroism, compassion, filial obedience, marital loyalty, the value of friendship and of love surmounting obstacles. Containing the teachings of ancient Hindu sages, the *Ramayana* is one of India's most important literary works and has been retold in poetic and theatrical versions by many of her greatest writers and artists.

In Cambodia, the influence of the *Ramayana* has been greater than any other story. It was translated and adapted as the *Reamker* by the Khmers in about the

17th century. The earlier origins of the *Reamker* are lost in time, but modern scholars agree that the Khmers used the threads of the *Ramayana*, or one of its many versions, localised it and translated it into a form used by local storytellers until it was formalised in a written text principally for the repertoire of the court, *lakhon preah reach troap*, and the classical dance, *lakhon luong*. It has been central to all forms of Cambodian theatrical repertoires since. As well as appearing as carved narratives at Angkor and in frescoes at other temples in Cambodia, it would have existed in text form, or a dramatic recitative, to be used for mimed performances of the Royal Ballet and safeguarded by ballet masters. These would now be impossible to trace[2]. A version published by the Institut Bouddhique in Phnom Penh in 1937, parts of which were translated into French by Saveros Pou, has been translated into English by Judith M Jacob. There is also a rare manuscript of the *Reamker* in the British Library dating from the late 19th century.

The Khmer version, adhering to the grandiose style of the original epic, is filled with battles, confrontations and emotional crises, with the divine and supernatural

dimensions always uppermost. At one time, performances might have lasted for as long as seven days, with particular episodes being danced for four-hour periods. Not restricted to aristocracy, however, oral versions became popular throughout the country, recited or sung by storytellers, in addition to dance and shadow puppet interpretations in villages as part of entertainments and spirit propitiation to mark festivals and auspicious events. A complete oral version was recorded in Siem Reap in 1969, according to David Chandler.

The extant version that is danced now is not complete. Although the characters in the *Reamker* remain in a mythical Indianised kingdom, the drama has been adapted to a Theravada Buddhist context, with Khmer ideology, psychology and language, as medieval Cambodia was steeped in Buddhist beliefs which coexisted syncretically with Hinduism and Brahmanism. The scenario, although based on the Hindu version, is therefore imbued with the teachings of the Buddha.

Preah Ream (Prince Rama in the original epic) is revered not just as a god but as the Buddha himself, possessing supernatural knowledge and constant integrity while fighting the forces of evil. Cambodian audiences have always felt a great empathy for Preah Ream and vicariously live his experiences, suffering his misfortunes and rejoicing in his pleasures, so that, from the start, an emotional relationship exists between the protagonist and spectator. The plot incorporates similar moral and emotional issues to the Indian version but is peopled by a Khmer *dramatis personae* of celestial spirits and malignant demons, kings and princesses, resplendent in extravagant costumes, whose colourful and comic adventures, especially in rural versions, alternate with the more serious strands of the story. Accompanying music for the performance is played by a classical orchestra and the story is narrated. The exaggerated, melodramatic language of the text is an interesting contrast to the slow, controlled steps of the balletic interpretation.

Above and below: **Little dancers enact the roles of Sovann Maccha and Hanuman.**

The Story of the Reamker

Preah Ream, born in Ayodhya (a kingdom of the Indian subcontinent), is the favourite son of King Dasaratha and much loved by the people. But he is exiled from the kingdom he was to have inherited as his stepmother, Kaikeyi, wants her own son, Bharata, second son of Dasaratha, to succeed to the throne. The Khmer version starts at this point, while the classical version opens earlier. The beautiful and virtuous Neang Seda (Sita), daughter of the king of Ayodhya, had been promised to 'the one who could bend Shiva's bow' and had thus became Preah Ream's wife.

With Neang Seda, Ream then flees his kingdom, taking with him his younger brother Preah Leak (Laksmana) into the forest of Dandaka where, over the next 14 years, they have numerous adventures. Preah Leak is the incarnation of the Naga on which Vishnu sleeps, and his loyalty and obedience to his brother are exemplary.

Seda's beauty arouses the lust of the wicked Krung Reab (Ravana), the ten-headed, twenty-armed king of the giants, or ogres, the Yaks, servant of the destructive aspect of the god Shiva, and ruler of Krong Langka. Blessed by Brahma after a penance, Reab supposedly cannot be killed by gods or demons. Reab's niece, Neang Surpanakha, a female demon, recently widowed, had tried to seduce Preah Ream whom she wanted for a husband. Preah Leak punished her by shaving her head. As revenge, Surpanakha encourages Reab's hatred for Ream by causing him to fall in love with Seda. His chance to abduct her comes one day when, in the forest, Seda sees a golden, bejewelled deer, which is in fact the demon Marica in disguise, and asks Ream to catch it for her. While Ream and Leak pursue the golden deer, Reab, disguised as an aged and devout Brahmin, seizes the opportunity to accost Seda, flatter her and then capture her, and carries her off to his kingdom on a flying magic chariot.

After Ream kills the golden deer with his arrow, and it metamorphoses into Marica, the disguised uncle of Reab, he is distraught at the disappearance of his wife. In the original epic, the passages in which Rama laments the loss of his treasured Sita and searches for 'the much loved, the wondrous fair one' comparing her to a sapphire, with a forehead that shines like the gold of a candleholder, eyes like precious corals and ears like golden flowers, are among the most beautiful passages in Indian literature and appear in the Khmer version. Grief-stricken, he sets out to find her.

To rescue Seda, Ream decides to attack the island of Krong Langka (Sri Lanka), where she is imprisoned in Reab's fortress. He is helped by Hanuman, the white monkey, brave, intelligent and supposedly immortal, son of the god of the wind, Vayu, whose speed he has inherited. Hanuman has magical powers, showing that the forces of nature are at his command. Together with Sugrib (Sugriva), a monkey general and ruler of the monkey kingdom, they offer to transform themselves into a bridge to Krong Langka, but Ream shoots a magic arrow that causes the sea to dry up so that they can cross to the island. The Khmer version contains episodes unique to Southeast Asian cultures, where Ream and Hanuman try to build a bridge to the island with stones only to have their efforts thwarted by the queen of the mermaids, Sovann Maccha. With her powerful entourage of fish and mythical sea creatures, she removes the stones. The monkeys capture the sea creatures, leaving Sovann Maccha alone in her watery realm where she is pursued by Hanuman. He courts her in a light-hearted scene, particularly popular with Cambodian audiences, where they dance together, at first argumentatively and then in amity, as he finally wins her over and she agrees to help construct the bridge.

Eventually reaching the island, Hanuman gains access to Krung Reab's fortress. Here, the hapless Seda has resisted the amorous advances of her captor who is so enraged that he has ordered two female demons to punish her. At this moment, Hanuman intervenes and manages to give Seda a ring belonging to Ream to prove that he is her husband's emissary, and repels the demons. Reab realises his fortress is on the brink of a siege and marshals his army to go and apprehend Ream. There follows a ferocious battle, with Hanuman and Sugrib fighting against the demons, Rakshasas, of wicked Preab. At the height of the drama, Ream and Preab fight a duel which culminates in Ream finally killing Reab.

After rescuing Seda, however, Ream will not take her back until she can prove, through an ordeal of fire (an alarming concept both here and in the Indian original as Seda has suffered so much throughout the epic), that she was not unfaithful to him while a prisoner for 14 years in Reab's palace. Neang Seda approaches the sacrificial fire while her attendants, holding candles, circle around, singing. However, her purity is such that that the gods come down to testify to her faithfulness and she emerges unscathed. Having proved her innocence, she is reunited with Ream, and they return in triumph to Ayodhya to reclaim the throne.

Royal couple in flying pose.

Above right: **Fight between Preah Ream and Krung Reab.**

Hanuman in a love pose.

Theories of good and evil are embodied in the four principal characters, the Prince, *neayrong*, the Princess, *neang*, the Giant, *yak*, and the Monkey, *sva*, three of which were traditionally played by females. The characters of the *Reamker* are prototypes, representing every aspect of humanity, not only as diverse personalities, but as the many aspects within one. Each displays human weaknesses and strengths ranging from jealousy, betrayal, lust, greed and envy to love, courage, mercy and forgiveness. But these sentiments are expressed with restraint, even amid battles. This is an art form in which modesty, grace and understatement are paramount and over-dramatisation is regarded as distasteful. Codes of behaviour and conduct valued in Cambodia thus emerge, such as gentleness and shyness in women and bravery and nobility in men. Ream and Seda represent the ideal couple, the perfect man and woman, demonstrating love in adversity, loyalty and fidelity. Ream also represents ideal manhood and kingship, while Seda is the epitome of feminine constancy and regal grace. Theirs is an intensely human story but the *Reamker* is also about the redemption of the world and, through religious devotion, of the individual. Infused with philosophy and mysticism, it is a universal tale, containing all the seeds of human wisdom, essentially creating a sense of order out of the chaos of existence.

The beauty of the *Reamker* in dance form is its balance of gravitas and humour. The role of the monkey, so close to human beings and yet lacking their rationality, intellect and soul, is a foil, similar to the fool in Shakespeare's plays. With his amusing, mischievous scampering, he provides a comic counter balance to the serious, holy plane of the drama. The monkey is a return to earth, to the mundane, bringing relief and laughter, before the audience is once again transported back to the metaphysical heights. But in the juxtaposition of people and animals, the monkeys are more than mere creatures. Hanuman and Sugrib are also semi-divine and, like Shakespeare's fools, expose the truth behind human façades. As soldiers of Preah Ream's army, they reflect the moral values and virtues of the royal leader for whom they are fighting. Cravath[3] believes that the monkey's role is ambivalent and adds that as all dualities are relative, Hanuman represents the intuitive, Feminine aspect of Ream as well as the rational Masculine principle.

It is the comical aspects of the monkeys that seize the audience's imagination and for rural spectators these are easier to grasp than the more intellectual, arcane depths of the drama, making it more accessible, giving them a sense that they have appreciated the epic. Producers of the *Reamker* in the countryside realised this and emphasised these scenes, playing to the house. Saveros Pou writes[4] that "we can confidently conclude that Valmiki's *Ramayana* as indigenized in Cambodia had a good grip on the popular mind and took on a quasi-magical aura that then swelled and increased in size and power to reach into other aspects of Khmer everyday life." The introduction of local concerns and political beliefs also gave the epic more immediacy. Yet this could also be manipulative since empathy with particular characters could blur the distinctions between the fictitious world of the drama and the real one of the audience. But dance productions of the *Reamker* always conclude with the celebration of the virtuous characters.

Some observers admit that it is difficult to understand the influence the *Reamker* has had for so long in Cambodia. But it is, perhaps, the familiarity of the story and the conflict of good and evil achieving a sense of balance that give it an enduring appeal. It is fundamentally optimistic. No matter how potent the force of evil in tempting human frailty, divine intercession is at hand. Because these stories are of supernatural beings and the manifestation of their sacred power, they also become the exemplary model for human

activity. Above all, the style of the *Reamker* provides an insight into the elegant and refined theatrical activity of Cambodia's past while providing a sense of continuity and reassurance in an uncertain present.

To have seen the *Reamker* performed at Angkor Wat or in the royal palace on the night of a full moon, unfolding by candlelight, must have been a magical experience that would have filled an audience with awe. Invoking the divine realm would have been just as palpable in a village production where parts of the *Reamker* were played at different times of the year as prayers. For example, when rains threatened to flood the country, the section where the monkey are trying to cross the water to Langka becomes especially symbolic. Conversely, if drought threatened, the section where Ream shoots a magic arrow and causes the seas to dry also takes on a more poignant and sacred aspect.

Various episodes of the *Reamker* have traditionally been played in different forms of dance-drama. Some are played in the court forms of female dance-drama, *lakhon kbach boran*. The all-male masked dance-drama, *lakhon kaol*, where verses are narrated by a chorus, who chant, while the actors dance, accompanied by music, is dedicated entirely to the epic, as is the shadow theatre, *sbek thom* and *nang sbaek*. *Lakhon kaol* was separate from the royal court. One of the most sacred and oldest of dance disciplines, it developed during the Angkorian era as a male version of

classical dance, with male actors playing the female roles as well. Pich Tum Kravel claims[5] that the genre emerged during the 13th-century religious conflicts. Angkor's exclusively female court dancers enjoyed rare privileges, but their proximity to power made them vulnerable. If female dancers were sacrificed during the turmoil, explains Kravel, it might have spawned a male version of the *Reamker* in which female roles were also taken by men. It became especially popular in the 1960s when there were at least 30 troupes performing it throughout the country.

Above and middle: **Two flying poses: Hanuman (middle), Krung Reab (above).**

Above far left: **Valin and Sugriva fighting in a scene from the *Reamker*, Angkor Wat.**

Makara dance. The first dancer represents the head of the monster, the last its tail. Fans suggest shimmering scales.

Sviey Andet, near Phnom Penh, was a village famed for its *lakhon kaol* troupe, which would come to the royal palace to perform. It was their talented monkey dancers who inspired Queen Kossamak to include similar performers to the royal troupe. Their New Year *lakhon kaol* performance of the *Reamker* was a profoundly spiritual ceremony, sometimes performed as a prayer for peace, but especially as a prayer for rain, and occasionally lasting as long as seven days. The New Year, *Chaul Cham*, in April, coincides with the wait for the start of the rainy season and the end of agricultural activity so that farmers could get involved with the performances of the *lakhon kaol*. The Wat Sviey Andet troupe owned a text of the *Reamker* that was kept in the monastery[6], inscribed on palm leaves and school exercise books. During the Pol Pot regime, the *wat* was used as a detention centre and none of these texts remain. Only seven members of this troupe survived. Now in their seventies, they have passed on what they can remember to young performers. *Kaol* has recently experienced a revival, in particular with a production of *Weyreap's Battle* which has been shown in Australia and England, notably at the Barbican theatre, where actors appeared in lavish, glittering costumes of gold spun silk that belied its rustic roots. This was the first fully staged *lakhon kaol* to be revived since the end of the Pol Pot regime.

Weyreap's Battle is an episode from the *Reamker* in which Preah Ream is abducted by Weyreap, an ogre or giant, who rules the underwater region of Badal. Hanuman sets out to rescue Preah Ream, facing a series of adventures, from battling aquatic creatures to transforming himself into a tiny insect so that he can rescue Ream from being plunged into boiling water. It features Hanuman's army of monkeys, playfully cartwheeling, leaping and swinging, scratching themselves shamelessly, much to the audience's amusement, while the sea creatures, sporting huge, waving claws in vivid colours and flashing eyes add a surrealistic flourish to the whole proceedings.

But behind the colourful humour, this dance-drama, once performed in villages and the countryside, features many important moral issues such as respect for elders, fidelity and heroism, as well as duplicity, betrayal and revenge. The scene where the masked monkey, Machanub, discovers that Hanuman is his father and is in conflict with Weyreap, his godfather, is especially moving as Machanub realises that to be loyal to one means betraying the other

Opposite: **Weyreap's Battle** by Heng Chivoan.

Em Theay praying before a rehearsal.

Dance rituals and prayers

Sampeah Kru

Preceding every performance there is a prayer of offering. This prayer to the *kru*, gurus or teachers of dance, honours the spiritual aspect of the relationship of the teacher and dancer (see Chapter History of Dance) who has passed on ancient traditions. Incense and candles are lit, flowers, offerings of food, rice, betel nut, lustral water and specially prepared floral displays with banana leaves are presented to honour the spirits of past teachers. These are placed on a low table along with costume masks, and *mkot,* which are each imbued with a spirit. The ceremony includes raising these offerings to salute the spirits. Dancers go through gestures of their ballets. Teachers close the ceremony by placing white cotton strings on the wrists of their pupils, an ancient tradition, while offering up prayers. Musicians perform a *homrong* to accompany these prayers.

The *sampeah* emulates the traditional form of salutation in Cambodia, the bow, with joined hands raised to the lips, once invested with myriad, subtle meanings depending upon whom one was greeting, as it would be accordingly lower, and more respectful, to people of distinction, such as royalty or religious figures. Formerly, the bow had been a ritual encoded with signals of class and respect. Cambodians would have never made physical contact with strangers, as in a hand-shake, such as they have adopted now, and it would have been unthinkable for a woman to touch a man.

Buong Suong

Ancient prayer rituals include the *buong suong*, meaning obeisance to female divinities, which lasts up to two hours and comprises four dances, two of which are solos. The Brahmanistic ceremony, with Buddhist and animistic overtones, invokes the aid of the gods, ancestral spirits and supernatural forces, the *neak ta*, to protect the kingdom, a ritual of making a promise of future offerings. *Buong suong*, claims Chheng Phon, sometimes accompanies the *tway kru* ceremony honouring the dance teacher. The *Buong Suong Tevoda* was first performed in the throne room of the palace.

The offering ceremony reinforces the sacred aspect of the ballet. It is performed every Thursday before performances and is also held to mark special occasions. Dancers believe that it ensures protection from the spirits. It is also a ritual of thanks for the teachers from whom the students have been honoured to learn.

A master of ceremonies, dressed in white, recites ritual texts in front of images of the gods, surrounded by offerings. The ballet masters and pupils prepare themselves spiritually and the orchestra plays the Satuka, a piece of music composed especially for the ceremony. Teachers then tie cotton threads around the wrists of their students, blessed with holy water, a symbolic way of bringing all the spirits back into the body.

A welcome dance is performed at one of the Angkorean temples.

Drawing of an offering ceremony by Sappho Marchal.

Chap robam

This *robam* is a welcome ceremony dance, one of several created by Queen Kossamak. Just as religious occasions were preceded by a sacred dance, so she choreographed a welcome dance, like an overture, before a theatrical performance. The warmth shown by the dancers as they scatter fragrant petals at the end is a fitting debut for the performers.

Robam Bach Phkar Choun Por

Recreated by Queen Kossamak, this ceremony by nine female dancers was performed as a royal blessing in which flower petals were thrown from a golden goblet to guests as a good luck gesture, *bai pka*, Tossing The Flowers.

Robam Phkar Meas Phkar Prak

This dance of Gold and Silver flowers, an opening dance performed by eight female dancers, was popular in the Sihanouk era. It evolved from the practice of offering silver and gold flowers as a political tribute that proliferated throughout Southeast Asia for centuries.

Ream Leak-Chhup Leak

An extract from the *Reamker*, resuscitated by Queen Kossamak.

Chap robam, or Welcome Ceremony dance.

Pamina Devi at Joyce Theatre, New York, 2007.

Apsara dance at Angkor Wat.

Pumtheara Chend in Pamina Devi at Joyce Theatre, New York, October 2007.

Robam Makara

Believed to have originated at the court of King Sisowath, *Robam Makara* was recreated in 1950 to include elements from an older, sacred dance-drama and incorporates characters from Khmer cosmology and legend. Vorachan, a deity, appears first to dance a solo. Then Moni Mekhala, goddess of the sea, appears, in her glittering, bejewelled gold costume and head-dress, with an entourage of attendants who manipulate fans to represent the shimmering scales of a mythical sea snake, the *makara*, as they move across the stage, curving in sinuous forms to emulate the snake's movements. The first dancer represents the head of the *makara*, which is always monstrous, while the last dancer in the row represents the tail.

Apsara Dance

Adapted by Queen Kossamak in 1962, this has come to be regarded as the ultimate classical dance, even though it is relatively recent. It was immortalised by Princess Buppha Devi, for whom it was originally choreographed. Originating from the delicate movements of the *apsaras* at Angkor, it is often performed as the opening dance of an event, and radiates an aura of sacred ritual in its slow, intense movements. Five *apsaras* descend from a temple *bas-relief*, and as the music of a *pin peat* orchestra starts, appear to come to life. They embody the elegance and radiance of the celestial spirits, devoid of human weaknesses and imperfections, enhanced by their stillness and calm. The music is accompanied by melodic vocals from singers who describe the life of the celestial dancers in their idyllic sylvan setting. The dancers finish with a traditional salutation, hands together and heads bowed, and as their dance comes to a close, they return to their carved niche. As the dream fades, only the stone *apsaras* remain. Queen Kossamak faithfully reproduced the head-dresses, jewellery and poses of the *apsaras*.

The Story of Mekhala

This is a symbolic story of the origins of thunder and lightning. Together they bring rain, imparting fertility and renewed life to the land. Dancers re-enact the battle between two mythical figures, Moni Mekhala, goddess and protector of the waters, wearer of a jewel encrusted belt, (*moni* means diamond and *mekhala* means belt, in Sanskrit and Khmer) charged with

rescuing shipwrecked people, and the giant, or ogre, Ream Eyso, a demon who controls storms and tries to steal her magic crystal.

The two protagonists are the acolytes of a hermit famed for his skills in magic, and each is charged to collect the morning dew as a contest with a prize.

To do this, the hermit gives each of them an empty glass. The following morning Ream Eyso ventures out at dawn, picks many leaves and squeezes them so that the drops of dew drip from each leaf into the container. Moni Mekhala, however, starts the night before, by leaving a handkerchief overnight on the grass. In the morning it is drenched in dew which she squeezes into the container. Thus, she is awarded the prize. The hermit takes her glass of morning dew and transforms it into a crystal ball, filled with magical powers. Ream Eyso is angry that the goddess has succeeded in winning the prize, but is given a magic axe by the hermit as consolation. The giant then goes in search of Moni Mekhala intent on stealing her crystal ball. The goddess, who retains her composure in the face of the stamping giant, distances herself gracefully. But he is so angry that he hurls his axe at her with such ferocity that the heavens shake. But he misses Moni Mekhala who throws her crystal ball into the air, creating lightning which blinds the giant, who falls to the ground.

The song that accompanies this performance at the moment of the encounter between Moni Mekhala and Ream Eyso was translated by ethnomusicologist Amy Catlin, in *Apsara: The Feminine in Cambodian Art*:

> "The costume is studded
> With shining golden flowers
> The belt shines brightly
> And the crown is very beautiful.
> The highest woman of the world
> Carried the magic diamond
> The powerful jewel
> And she leaves her kingdom
> She dodges and parries and circles around,
> Waving the diamond up and down,
> Blinding the eyes of the giant
> Until he falls."

Moni Mekhala glides away; Ream Eyso recovers, regains his sight, and disappears into the clouds.

Every new year, the confrontation between Moni Mekhala and Ream Eyso is re-enacted at festivities throughout the country and when Cambodians see the

Above and below: **The *Apsara* dance immortalised by Princess Buppha Devi remains a perennial favourite.**

Above and below: **Young dancers perform a fan dance.**

offer thanks to the gods. It was adapted by Queen Kossamak from a dance for two, a princess and prince, to a piece for twelve dancers.

Robam Bopha Lokey, Earth Flower Dance
This is a classical dance, performed by girls who represent flowers. It is often performed on ceremonial occasions and on International Childrens' Day.

Monorea
The tale of Preah Sothon Neang Monorea, a legend from the non-canonical *jataka* tales, was restored during Princess Buppha Devi's tenure as Minister of Culture and dedicated to Queen Kossamak who created a shortened version of this dance. It was shown in December 2003. It recounts the tale of a celestial princess, Neang Monorea, and her six sisters in their heavenly abode. Faithful to the Hindu concept whereby feminine grace is a mirror of celestial beauty, the dance celebrates the mythical aura of the heavenly dancers who embody idealised female attributes. Each possesses a magical scarf which enables them to fly away. They ask their father's permission to visit earth and, when he agrees, they descend and bathe in a lotus pond. Unbeknownst to them, a prince, Preah Sothon, out hunting, is secretly watching them. When the sisters fly back home, at the sound of a gong, Neang Monorea cannot find her scarf. She remains behind and Preah Sothon offers to help her find it. They fall in love, marry and go to live in his palace.

Sothon's country is invaded and his father insists he must go to war. During his absence his mother is told by a fortune teller that to avenge her sins from a previous life, and to save her son during the war, Neang Monorea must die. Rather than kill her, they send her into exile. She meets a hermit as she makes her way back to her former home, and gives him a ring to give to her husband. On his return, the prince is heartbroken to find her gone and goes in search of her. He finds the hermit who gives him the ring. After many adventures, he reaches his beloved's celestial world. By dropping the ring into a waterpot being replenished for the princess's bath by celestial maidens, he makes himself known to her. She goes to the spot where he awaits her, they are reunited and her parents allow him to stay with her in their heavenly realm.

dark thunder clouds gathering in the sky, they believe that the goddess and the demon will engage in their eternal battle and flood the rice fields. This is a dance to call for rain, praying to the spirits to bestow their blessings. At a deeper level, it may be seen as illustrating the difference between ignorance and enlightenment.

Sovann Maccha
Queen of the Fish, and daughter of Reab, Sovann Maccha is one of the most popular dramatic dances in the repertoire. The mermaid Sovann Maccha obstructs Hanuman's plan to construct a causeway to the island of Langka to rescue Seda. Each time one of his monkeys lays a stone, her fish removes them. But he seduces her into helping the monkeys, with her fellow mermaids, to build a stone bridge to the island of Langka to save Seda who is a prisoner of the giant demon Reab. The duet between Hanuman and Sovann Maccha is full of wit and humour, by turns coquettish and seductive.

Robam Tep Monoram
Another favourite dance created by Queen Kossamak in which the dancers ask the gods to transform them into *apsaras*. Their prayer is answered after which they

Rural Dances

A number of rural dances, originating in country festivities, such as harvest festivals, were incorporated into the canon of dance at RUFA during the 1960s. These lighthearted dances have remained popular and are performed frequently for tourists. The steps and movements are simple and lack the sophistication and refinement of court dance.

Coconut Dance, Robam Kuoh Tralok

This popular folk dance from Svay Rieng province is performed at wedding ceremonies as a game. Using coconut shells as castanets, the dancers punctuate their movements with shouts. It is a playful performance, expressing joy and harmony. The dance was directed by Chheng Phon during the 1960s and became part of the curriculum of the Royal University of Fine Arts in 1966. Costumes for this and other folk dances are much simpler than those for classical dance. The dancers wear cotton clothes, similar to those worn in the countryside, such as shirts, loose trousers, and a check scarf, *krama*, sometimes knotted around the head.

Fishermen's Dance, Robam Naesat

Cambodia is rich in fish from the Tonle Sap lake and the Mekong River. This dance, performed at Khmer New Year and ceremonial occasions, is another rural dance by boys and girls, dressed in simple cotton outfits holding their fishing baskets, in a courtship ritual. The girl is shy and the boy is bold, and it demonstrates attitudes to love and courtship. In its atmosphere of innocence, it alludes to the rural values of women in traditional roles, avoiding scandals, and preparing for family life. Theatrical folk dances like these were taught at the Royal University of Fine Arts and this one was choreographed in 1967 by Vann Sun Heng, under the supervision of Professor Chheng Phon.

Tbal kadeung

A rice harvest dance, with girls reprimanding boys for abandoning their work to drink palm juice. Another playful and flirtatious dance of the countryside, it also has an underlying message of the traditions of relationships between boys and girls.

Robam Kangaok Pailin

The Peacock Dance from Pailin is danced by two performers in glittering turqoise peacock costumes.

Legend relates that a princess dreams that a peacock presents a Buddhist sermon. When she falls ill, a hunter brings a male peacock who will recite the Buddhist prayers in return for being liberated. The princess frees him and he returns on Buddhist holy days. The dancers flutter and strut to capture the peacock's exotic movements. The dance invokes the rain spirits, as the peacock in Khmer mythology has special powers and represents royal grace and wisdom, qualities enhanced by the bird's splumage which appears to have images of eyes on its tail feathers. It is performed on holidays and Independence Day to bring prosperity to villagers, and it accompanies ritual ceremonies to pray for rain. The dance was choreographed by Professor Chheng Phon and Professor Pol Som Oeurn in 1965 and now forms part of the curriculum at the Royal University of Fine Arts.

Duel

Duel, choreographed by King Norodom Sihamoni (when still a prince), had its debut in April 1995 at the Chaktomuk Theatre in Phnom Penh. Influenced by Russian choreography, it gives a more important role to male dancers. It opens with an exquisite solo by a female dancer, performing ritualised movements by candlelight. She then pauses to witness a combat between two men, symbols of the prehistoric social and religious duality of her civilisation. The *Duel* is a dramatic symbiosis of Western and Khmer dance and the ballet, with overtones of Russian dance and ideas from choreographers such as Pina Bausch, resonates with the tension of duality, as East meets West. "All my ballets reflect these themes," the prince told me at the time. "I am a child of two cultures and I can never dissociate myself from that. So it is always the theme of my work." He added: "There is something of *L'Après-midi d'un Faune* in *Duel*. Khmer dance is very sensual, even though it is sacred. Look at the dancers' feet, as they touch the ground, slowly the skin makes contact, the women move sensuously."

The piece, accompanied by classical Khmer music, was received by a rapturous audience and the theatre's 600 seats overflowed into the aisles and spectators called for encore after encore.

King Sihanouk bought 200 tickets for each of the two following performances and gave them all away.

Boys and girls perform the coconut dance.

A scene from *Duel*.

Kbach representing gathering a flower and benediction.

Kbach, hand gesture symbolising a leaf: *kbach oung due*.

Above and below: ***Kbach troung*** symbolising a bud.

Kbach Oung Due symbolising a leaf.

The Gestures of Cambodian Dance

The *kbach* are the standard hand gestures of classical dance, performed at a slow, hypnotic pace, co-ordinated with synchronised sculptural poses that are infused with serenity and equilibrium. The nuanced gestures of the hands gain their meaning from the entire movement of the body. The word *kbach* means cadence. It implies a sequence to the movements as well as the beat or measure of rhythmic motion, and can refer to the body in dynamic action or in static pose. A pose held immobile for a time is preceded by a series of almost imperceptible gestures which then give way to more rapid steps. The significance of each gesture is determined by the one that precedes it and the one that follows it, like a phrase of music. *Kbach rongvael* is a slow cadence, while *kbach banchos* is faster, and each takes about three months to learn. *Kbach lea* is a departing cadence, executed at the close of a scene, while *kbach choet* is a rapid walk and *kbach smeu* is for exits and entrances. A circular step performed by a divinity is a *kbach mul* and a combat pose is the *kbach chhoet chhung*.

These myriad slow movements conform to a precise language, with its own vocabulary, syntax and punctuation and their sequence determines a meaning that emerges in the context of the dance. The exact number of gestures is not certain, but more than 8,000 photographs have been taken by scholars such as William Lobban, to record the nuances of these subtle gestures. Encoded in the form and technique of every movement are symbols and meanings that resonate for dancers and for audiences who share their values.

Symbolises the leaf.

Symbolises the bud.

Symbolises the fruit.

Symbolises the stem.

Symbolises the flower in bloom.

Gestures combine to have other meanings. *Kbach sung luc* and an upside down *kbach cheap* and turning back to *kbach sung luc* may mean a beckoning gesture.

When rehearsals of all these movements are complete, dancers are then ready to prepare themselves for the invocation to the spirits, *Pithi Sampeah Kru Lakhon Krop Muk*, whereupon their teachers deem this the right moment to put on their masks. This forms part of the special *boung soung* ceremony on Thursdays.

As Cambodia does not appear to have had a dance manual comparable to the *Natya Sastra*, the legacy of these movements depends on oral transmission. Each generation copies the exact patterns from their predecessors so that they are never lost. Trained from early childhood by ballet masters, the pupils, like those of the West, are often subjected to extreme positions into which they force their bodies while still pliable and supple. The arms need to be flexible. When lifted, they train their arms to become so straight that the elbow joint is thrown into an inverted bend, and as they move, the arm flexes and straightens continuously. The dancers appear almost double jointed. When the arms are raised, the elbow should be higher than the shoulder in the feminine roles and only slightly higher in the vigorous masculine roles.

The legs are permanently flexed at the knees for almost the entire dance, and the students must perfect their sense of balance, learning to stand and to turn on one leg and rotate in a slow, measured movement like an arabesque, each step a meditation, while the arms and hands go through their series of gestures, their wrists and fingers moving imperceptibly slowly in statuesque stillness. Feet are turned slightly out, with the toes lifted. This gives a visual illusion of lightness, even though the dancer is firmly grounded. The heel of the supporting foot also alternately rises and falls again to the floor. A rapid beating of the feet on the floor signifies emotion and a thump of the heel shows anger or decision. In masculine roles, rapid bourrées in the classical ballet position of *plié en seconde* are used a mode of progression in scenes portraying battles.

Above right and far right: **Two poses signifying love: for the male performer both feet remain on the ground, for the woman one foot is raised.**

Detail showing feet movements and flexed knees. Pamina Devi, Joyce Theatre, New York.

For a female dancer, the upper torso is held straight and regal, shoulders square, the neck long, the head moving slightly from side to side, while the back is arched in a deep, exaggerated curve, an unnatural posture that is practised and perfected from a young age, while the knees are bent, with the body firmly grounded and solidly anchored to the floor – similar to Japanese and Javanese theatrical forms. The expressive language is through the elaborate, hyperextended gestures of the hands. Male dancers are often in the *grand plié* position, a deep knee bed with feet rotating out, in a geometric shape of perfect symmetry. The *plié* is a smooth and continuous bending and straightening of the knees, almost like fencing, the stylised art of attack and defense with a sword or foil in a duel, with both swordsmen on bended knees, ready to spring or pounce. Rigid physical training is required to adapt the body to the exigencies of style, as the postures are the result of years of discipline.

The face does not reveal the emotions that inspire the movements. Unlike dance in Bali, for example, where eye movements and facial gestures increase the drama, in Cambodian dance the face remains serene, as if in meditation, seeming to echo the practice of remaining calm and unemotional in contact with other people, a centuries-old art of social interaction throughout Asia. Thus the spirit of the dancer, who is almost contemplative in her stillness and self control, flows down to the hands, whose graceful, elegant gestures communicate symbols and values to an audience that understand them. The body slowly follows where the hands lead. This stillness impressed the poet Rainer Maria Rilke[7] who described the dancers as 'metamorphosed gazelles'. Their hands recalled those of the Buddha, he wrote, for they know "how to sleep … to rest for centuries on laps … reclaiming infinite silence."

To enhance this sense of immobility, Cambodian dance, in common with other Asian forms, places emphasis on the quality of being grounded. This is a contrast to Western dance that is almost defiant of gravity as male dancers leap ever higher, seemingly lighter and lighter, in athletic feats that render the body superhuman, with female dancers *sur la pointe* in block ballet slippers. Although the ideal Cambodian dancer is as graceful, slender and fine-boned, Cambodian dance asserts the importance of gravity. Dancers are anchored to the floor, with knees bent, feet stamping, and descend increasingly lower, in contact with the earth, sometimes sinking completely to the ground until the dance is performed in a seated position. While Western dance is a tribute to speed and lightness, rising vertically, Cambodian dance is a celebration of slowness, as if arresting the process of time, sinking horizontally. This reflects the concept of the body for the Khmers. It is sacred and not to be displayed in leaping and pirouetting or any action that would diminish composure. Like the *apsaras*, the body must be serene, static and without expression.

The slowness and repetition of Cambodian dance is as much a source of criticism as praise. Geoffrey Gorer[8] admitted that after seeing the Cambodian dancers at the Colonial Exhibition in Paris he was initially impressed. "I still think their 'lifting' movement

Above: **Dancer in full costume.**

Dancers sink to the floor in seated posture.

on one bent leg so that the whole body seems to be raised into the air very impressive." But he concluded, " their whole performance, with their white makeup, their expensive and peculiar costumes, and their stylised movements, is far pleasanter when seen in a European theatre. And they gain nothing by repetition."

By contrast, the style and pace of Oriental dance was praised by Havelock Ellis[9]. "The most beautiful dance I have ever seen was the slowest". Although referring to Javanese dance, his remarks apply equally to Cambodian dance: "The movements are so controlled that one posture flows imperceptibly into another. The rhythm is that of Nature herself – as clouds drift across a summer sky, constantly changing form; as waves of a tranquil sea swell and subside; as a flower opens, and slowly fades; as the sun, moon, planets and stars rotate in their orbits; as the four seasons succeed one another through eternity." The slowness of Cambodian dance recalls not only Javanese but other Asian forms such as the classical Noh theatre of Japan, which has a strong component of dance, with its stylised gestures, masked actors, restrained feeling and intensely still, contemplative atmosphere.

The seeming monotony of Cambodian dance was appreciated by dance critic Valerian Svetloff[10] who admired the "beautiful plastic design which gradually emerges to the sound of a soothing, lulling rhythm." He was captivated by the softness of Cambodian dance, "much of it a sort of noontide languor. It is as if the heat and the sun and the blue skies of Indo-China had stamped their indelible mark on these placid dances…" Cambodian ballet was not so much a technically-perfected choreographic art, he noted, as a "pantomimic drama in the antique sense, i.e. a series of stage pictures in which dancing forms an integral part of the dramatic action…"

This impression was reinforced by Xenia Zarina[11] who analysed the beauty of monotony "where imperceptible change is revealed, conveying a feeling of eternity, and the effect on the spectator is hypnotic".

For the Khmer audience, none of these analyses are necessary as they respond so profoundly to the sense of imperceptible change and slowness that they replicate it, with all the hand gestures, in their own dances at weddings and parties and absorb its rhythms as part of their own soul.

Thus mesmerised, the spectators, in suspended disbelief, have entered the divine realm of the sacred performance. They have experienced what Peter Brooke[12] called the Holy Theatre, the Theatre of the Invisible-Made-Visible, where the arts talk of patterns which we can only begin to recognise when they manifest themselves as rhythm or shapes. They have participated in the celebration of the gods.

Drawing by Sappho Marchal from *Danses Cambodgiennes*.

[1] On the southwestern wall, the Battle of Kurukshetra.

[2] Judith M Jacob, *Reamker*, Royal Asiatic Society, 1986.

[3] Paul Cravath, *Earth in Flower: The Divine Mystery of Cambodian Dance Drama*, 2008.

[4] *Indigenization of Ramayana in Cambodia*, Saveros Pou, reprinted 2003.

[5] Pich Tum Kravel in article by Robert Turnbull.

[6] William Lobban, *The Revival of Masked Theatre in Cambodia*, 1990.

[7] Rainer Maria Rilke letter to his wife in *Rodin and the Cambodian Dancers*, 2006.

[8] Geoffrey Gorer, *Bali and Angkor*, 1936.

[9] Havelock Ellis, *The Dance of Life*, 1923.

[10] Valerian Svetloff, *The Dancing Times*, 1932.

[11] Xenia Zarina, *Classic Dances of the Orient*, 1967.

[12] Peter Brooke, *The Empty Space*, 1968.

CHAPTER 10 MUSIC

Pin peat drums.

Drawing of the *pin peat* orchestra by Sappho Marchal.

"This music is like a the sound of a stream, a sound of water flowing … this is what creates the ethereal, dreamy and delicate atmosphere that unfolds around the movement of dance."
Samdach Chaufea Thiounn, *Danses Cambodgiennes.*

The traditional Khmer orchestra, *pin peat*, which accompanies all classical dance performances, shadow theatre, all male dance-drama and temple rituals, is an ensemble of wind, string and percussion instruments. The music is based on the polyphonic (many-toned) stratification of several musical lines, and is hetero-phonic, with simultaneous variations of a melody, founded primarily on a pentatonic, a five-tone, scale rather than the heptatonic, the seven-tone, scale used in Western music. It is constructed linearly and has no harmony in the Western sense. Ornamentation or embellishment is a characteristic feature of Khmer music. Instrumentalists playing together will have a collective melody in mind, but improvise it individually. The quality of a piece results from their knowledge and ability to perform it creatively. As music is an oral tradition, the players rarely use notation and composers are not usually known.

Khmer orchestras use a range of instruments, all made of indigenous materials, embellished with inlaid décor, including pipes, oboes, buffalo horns, flutes, fiddles, dulcimers, lutes, zithers, xylophones, gongs,

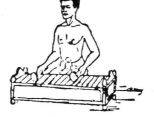

Carrying *pin peat* drums down from Angkor Wat.

Musicians at the court of King Norodom, Fonds Iconographiques des Missions Étrangères de Paris.

Below: **Playing the *tro Khmer*.**

Bottom: **The *kong thom*.**

drums and cymbals. With clashing cymbals, clanging gongs and a complicated drum beat holding it together, orchestral Khmer music has a distinctive and haunting character. By contrast, solo and duet music is quite delicate and plaintive.

Vocals feature significantly and the singers are usually female, while instrumentalists are male. The singers, with high pitched voices, accompany the music, chanting the narrative, and sometimes the dialogue. They are usually placed to the right hand side of the orchestra.

The classic orchestra is composed of two xylophones, *roneat*, a trough-resonated keyboard percussion instrument, played with two mallets, of which the *roneat ek*, is the smaller, higher pitched, with 21 wooden or bamboo keys, and the *roneat thung* the larger, lower pitched with sixteen wooden or bamboo keys. The *roneats* are usually played in tandem, with one playing a melody in octaves and the other weaving variations around the central theme. The music of the xylophone rises and falls and the drums start and stop on the half beats.

The *kong thom*, is a large semicircular arrangement of 16 flat gongs, and the *kong toch* is a small semicircle of gongs. The *som poh* are two circular sets of 19 gongs,

Pin peat orchestra. Front left is a *krapeu*, the woman at right plays a *tro Khmer*. Two *roneats* are in the middle ground, while a *kong thom* is propped against a pillar in the background. Photo: Pierre Dieulefils.

one of which is a treble instrument, the other a bass, tuned in sympathy with one another and producing elaborations on the main melody.

Wind instruments include the Khmer flute, *khloy*, a vertical duct flute made of bamboo, hardwood or plastic, with a buzzing membrane, one of the most popular instruments. In the countryside, a boy herding or watching his cattle will play such flutes. It has six or seven fingerholes and a thumbhole. The *pey pork* is a bamboo side-blown single free-reed pipe, with seven fingerholes and one thumbhole with a range of an octave. The smaller free reed, *sneng*, is made of water buffalo or ox horn with a single free reed. The oboe, *srelai*, is a hardwood quadruple-reed oboe. There are two sizes, each with a range of two octaves. The horn, *saeng*, is a conch shell horn.

String instruments comprise the *krapeu* (see page 117) a long wooden, fretted floor zither with three strings, in the shape of a crocodile – *krapeu* means crocodile in Khmer. Another plucked fretted lute is the *chapei dang veng*. There are also fiddles, *tro*. The *tro Khmer* is a three-stringed vertical spike fiddle with

coconut shell body, used in classical music. The *tro Khmer* is played with the bow loose, unattached to the strings. Strings are now made of metal but used to be silk. There are two two-stringed vertical fiddles with hardwood bodies, the *tro sau toch* and *tro sau thom*, both used in classical music.

Drums set the rhythm for all the musicians and are among the most important Khmer instruments. They are made up of the *sampho*, a double-headed barrel drum, which has a 'male' and 'female' voice, set horizontally on a stand, played with the heel of the palm of the hands; bass drums, the *skor*, a pair of large barrel drums played with sticks; the *thon*, a goblet shaped drum played with the hands; and a *rumana*, a frame drum, also played with the hands. The drums are identical to those depicted on carvings at the temples of Angkor. The drum is believed to have a spirit, and is kept in a special box. It is also considered unlucky to step over any instrument as to do so would break the connection with the spirits. Music has all the sacred resonance of dance.

The *sampho* is tuned by placing a ball of glutinous rice paste in the middle of the drum. The pressure alters the sound emanating from the tight skin pulled across the drum. Weight is put on the drumskin to slow down the vibration and deepen the tone. A fresh ball of rice is used for every performance and kept on for its duration. In some countries, beeswax and melted tar are used to tune the gongs which, when placed underneath, alter the pitch.

There are *chhing*, small brass cymbals and *chap*, flat cymbals, and clappers, *krap*. *Chhing*, found throughout Southeast Asia, are either tied together with a piece of cord and allowed to vibrate, or else they are stopped with a finger, which makes a ringing tone. This is the sound that co-ordinates the dances in classical ballet. In Western ballet, dancers may typically follow a melody or phrase. But here the musicians follow the dancers and, if necessary, they will extend the piece accordingly. The control of the steps comes from the *chhing* and the *srelai*.

In addition to the *pin peat*, there is the *phleng kar*, or wedding ensemble, the *korng skor*, a drum and gong group for funerals and the *arak*, that plays for spirit worship and communication. A *mohori* ensemble is for entertainment at folk dances and banquets with a repertoire that encompasses everything from love songs to lullabies. *Phleng mohori*, is a kind of secular chanting and a refined, nostalgic court music, usually played by a *pin peat*, performed for the king with the royal ballet. The word *mohori* is said to derive from a legendary singer named Monohori. Traditionally, there would be *chrieng chapei*, a story that is chanted and accompanied by the *chapei dong veng*, the two stringed, long necked guitar that the singer uses with his songs. It is often improvised.

Singer Kong Nay is the leading *chapei* performer in Cambodia. A master musician, he is blind and wears large dark glasses, and as a result has become known as the 'Ray Charles' of Cambodia. *Chapei* blends easily with other, modern musical forms and Kong Nay's performances often end up with everybody dancing.

The *chrieng tar* is an improvised secular ballad sung by men and women. *Ayai* is a sung comedy, usually performed by a boy and a girl who improvise a verbal duet. *Arak* is one of the oldest and finest musical genres in Cambodia, said to be 2,000 years old, pre-dating Hindu and Buddhist influences, and handed down through the generations. Played in sacred exorcism ceremonies it is used in sickness to appease and invoke the spirits of ancient Khmer civilisation and for prayers for physical and spiritual wellbeing. The rituals, usually conducted by elderly performers between 50-80 years old, will be followed by a Khmer orchestra.

Marriage songs, *phleng kar*, resonate with the memory of ancient *arak*. The *kar* ensemble is made up of seven wind, string and percussive instruments, with vocals. These ensembles are found throughout Cambodia. Formerly imbued with sacred overtones and used as a benediction, the *kar* ensemble was traditionally made up only of older musicians. The *kar* play for weddings, which last three days and nights, with the continuous music now broadcast over huge loudspeakers at top volume. These seem to be an essential part of many musical arrangements now, transforming the ethereal, dreamy sound once so evocative of Khmer music.

Music lesson on a *krapeu*.

Playing for a shadow puppet performance. The *sampho* in the foreground sets the rhythm. (PP)

CHAPTER 11 SHADOW PUPPETS

"Khmer people … love this story that shows the magnificent powers of the superheroes they adore. While listening to the chanting, their minds drift away and land on a celestial planet where grandiose events take place, great struggles between the good and the bad …"
Pich Tum Kravel, *Sbek Thom: Khmer Shadow Theatre*

Candles flicker in the dark and magical shadows move across a white screen. As the music starts, the adventures of mythical demons and goddesses, heroes and villains, epic battles, magic spells and unrequited love unfold. The tales are recounted by five or six puppeteers who are concealed behind the screen which is illuminated by candles or small fires. The puppeteers manipulate the shadow puppets so that the silhouette is visible from the other side. The puppeteers may even periodically make an appearance. Narrators stand in front, giving information, helping the spectators, who are seated on the ground on mats, to understand what is unfolding.

Shadow puppet shows are not just for children but for audiences of all ages. The shadows create a sense of mystery and divine inspiration, having their roots in religious observances. They are considered sacred, embodying Brahmanism and Buddhism. The art of the puppeteer developed from animistic beliefs that every object has a soul, so puppets are treated with reverence, as receptacles of living energy. Prayers and offerings precede each performance, accompanied by music, as the puppeteers ask for blessings and protection and pay homage to their teachers.

The drama is usually episodes from the *Reamker*, and the *jatakas*, the stories of the lives of the Buddha. Interspersed with these are numerous comic scenes, full of slapstick humour, inspired by rural life that, like fables, offer a moral reflection on the nature of existence.

Left and opposite above: **Performers hold up the large leather puppets, *sbek thom*, against a large sheet which glows orange from the light of the fire blazing behind. (PP)**

Making offerings before the show. (PP)

The origins of shadow theatre in Cambodia are obscure and even Pich Tum Kravel admits that they are unknown. A tradition throughout Asia, especially in Indonesia with its *wayang kulit*, in Japan with *bunraku* and in India where it once flourished, they exist in two forms in Cambodia, *sbek thom*, large perforated leather puppets, a classical form with religious origins, and *sbek touch*, small leather puppets, popular in the countryside and village shows. They are made up of figures cut from dried cow hide. The *sbek touch*, the smaller ones, are articulated, their arms being moved with sticks. The *sbek thom*, the larger ones, weighing up to eight kilos, are not moveable and are not, strictly speaking, puppets. According to Hang Soth there are three kinds of puppets, the third type, *sbek thom mothium*, is painted different colours and is used for marriages and funerals.

The normal set of puppets has 154 characters, and there may be as many as 300 in a troupe. They are referred to as 'hides'. Often the most important characters may be represented in three different postures, walking, fighting and sitting. Innumerable secondary

puppets representing birds and animals, houses and trees and even cars, aeroplanes and bombs, add to the drama and sometimes frenzied pace of the stories, accompanied by cymbals and drums. One of the most popular excerpts from the *Reamker* in the pre-war years was a battle on the island of Langka between Preah Ream and Preah Leak with Enthachit, son of Krung Reab, that would often take four or five nights to perform.

It takes three weeks to create one puppet. Fresh cow skin is soaked in a solution of tree bark and water, cured and stretched out tightly on a frame and dried in the sun for two weeks, so the process can only be done in the dry season. The outline of the puppet is cut using a special, thick knife and the minute details carved out with a chisel and a hammer. They are usually copied from a master stencil and are highly stylised. When the cutting is finished the moveable arms are attached and the puppet painted. Lines are drawn and accentuated with black ink.

The art of the puppeteer involves not only the fabrication and manipulation of the figures but also a

A fire of coconut husks lights up the sheet against which the puppets are held. (PP)

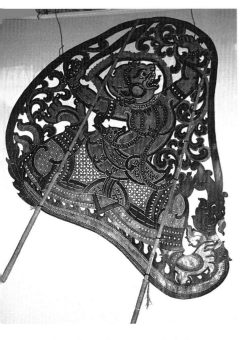

A medium size puppet, *sbek thom,* is painted with different colours.

The small puppets, *sbek touch,* are articulated.

prodigious memory to re-enact a considerable reper-toire of stories. The puppeteers need to be familiar with all the characters, frequently changing their voices. In *sbek thom*, the narrator is the principal performer, structuring and leading, editing and arranging the show.

Siem Reap has always been a centre for puppet production and performance where temples, such as Wat Raja Bo, are the venue for shows and repository of the puppets. They are always kept in a special shed that faces the sunrise, with a spirit house in front of it.

Pich Tum Kravel was responsible for saving puppet theatre in the 1970s and took a set of 147 shadow puppets to the National Theatre in Phnom Penh which he hid before the onset of the Pol Pot regime. Years later, Pich Tum Kravel and Hang Soth found a few of them, scattered around, while others have been brought back to them. "Pol Pot didn't know what to do with them. He didn't know how to manipulate puppets," observed Hang Soth ironically. Another group in Siem Reap, led by Duk Roeun, hid most of their 120 puppets in a hole in a tree which were recovered by survivors years later. Donations from bodies such as the French Embassy, who gave $8,500 in the early 1990s, helped towards making a whole new set.

Among the best *sbek thom* troupes in Siem Reap now are the Sala Kaseing Sbek Thom Troupe and the Angkor Sbek Touch Troupe. Phnom Penh's National Theatre Company of Cambodia has three troupes, the Sbek Touch Troupe, the Sbek Thom Troupe and the Sbek Por Troupe which has revived *sbek por*, a version

that is smaller than *sbek thom*. These talented groups tour the country.

Another inspiring shadow puppet centre in Phnom Penh is at the Souvanna Phum theatre on street 360, run by Mann Kosal (see Chapter 8). A survivor of the Pol Pot regime, 45-year-old Mann Kosal toured internationally as a shadow puppeteer in Ong Keng Sen's *Continuum: Beyond the Killing Fields*. "Now I find it too emotional and too traumatic to perform," he admitted.

At Souvanna Phum he uses classical and folk forms with all three sizes of puppets and performs shows almost every night. From the moment he first saw shadow puppetry in 1991, he loved it and imme-diately sold his motorbike for $400 to buy materials to make the puppets. He trained at the Royal University of Fine Arts and at the Tonle Bassac theatre and took over Souvanna Phum in the early 1990s when it was a theatrical venue known as the Magic Circus. He realised that shadow puppets also appeal to foreign visitors. The Souvanna Phum has a magical atmosphere which is palpable from the moment one enters. Every night it is filled with children, many of them orphans, all of whom come in free of charge. Mann Kosal's own two children are often among them. He has channelled all his energy into recreating this enchant-ing art form that captivates everyone, from the youngest child to the oldest grandparent, and is an introduction to the stories and myths which are the heart of Cambodia's spiritual foundations.

Above: **The well-detailed small cottage and tree form a delightful backdrop against which the story unfolds.**

Top: **The articulated puppets, *sbek touch*, usually tell stories from the *jataka* tales.**

Left: **Performance artists manipulating articulated puppets, *sbek touch*.**

CHAPTER 12 DANCE CLASSES

A class at the Royal University of Fine Arts Dance School (RUFA).

*"I believe that we learn by practice. Whether it means to learn to dance by practising dancing or to learn to live by practising living, the principles are the same …
One becomes in some area an athlete of God,"*
Martha Graham, *I Am A Dancer.*

Dance Training

Dance classes start at 7 am at the Royal University of Fine Arts, before the heat of day, in the open-sided halls built at Russei Keo, the new campus. This rather bleak neighbourhood, nine kilometres northwest of Phnom Penh, is where the dance school has been forced to move amid the controversial selling of their former premises in the city.

Several of the classes are all girls, aged from six to 17 years old, dressed in tight pink satin bodices, *aaw nay*, and red *sampot chawng kbun,* part sarong, part trousers, that enhance their long slender limbs and supple bodies. With bare feet, they move gracefully through their exercises, backs arched, knees flexed, while their hands, with fingers bent right back, unfold

Drawing by Sappho Marchal from one of the Halls of Dancers.

like flowers. They move at the slow, hypnotic pace of classical dance, with carefully synchronised steps, while their faces remain impassive, as they train their hands in all the graceful choreographed routine of gestures, the *chha banchos*, the 'mother poses.' These rigorous and demanding exercises, like those at the *barre* in classical Western dance, constitute the main movements of dance and take up to two hours to practise. Just as watching Western dancers warm up and practise in a studio gives one an insight into movement and a sense of how it is formulated, before admiring the perfect product on stage, so with the Cambodian dancers, as they stretch and bend. They are like a vision of heavenly beauty and, indeed, many of them will learn the dance of the *apsaras*, imitating the celestial dancers carved on the walls of Angkor Wat.

Only 70 students are selected a year at the school out of hundreds of hopefuls. Essential physical attributes for students are suppleness and grace as well as a slender but strong body. "Selecting children for the dance school is like a cattle market," Bill Lobban, the musicologist who worked with them in 1990s, told me. "Their legs, hands and even their teeth are examined to make sure they will be exactly right."

They start training at the age of five years old, learning exercises designed to stretch and manipulate joints, such as bending their fingers right back to touch the forearm, twisting and arching the waist and lying prone on the ground with legs crossed in the lotus position, a gymnastic exercise that demands discipline. Soth Somaly teaches 130 girls each day, coaxing their agile bodies into these seemingly impossible movements. The positions are held for long periods to increase muscle power, suppleness and flexibility. Like Western ballet, great demands are made on the body and require an ability to overcome the physical discomforts. From the age of ten, girls learn the basic vocabulary of gestures and poses. After completing this stage of training they are taught the repertory of non-narrative group dances. Students will then graduate to training for one particular dance role, depending on their physique and aptitude. Small girls with delicate

frames and round faces learn the female characters. Those who are slightly bigger-boned, with longer faces, learn the male roles, as they need a broader stance and bolder movements. Those with exceptionally supple bodies, but less pretty faces, are cast in the monkey roles of the *Reamker*, or else the ogres, or giants, masked characters whose dancing requires a wide, high-kneed gait.

Students lie on the floor in the lotus position to increase flexibility.

Tutors from the Apsara Arts Association, Vong Metry and Chhay Sopha.

It takes at least twelve years to train a dancer. Part of that time is dedicated to spiritual as well as physical preparations. To dance is to enter a sacred state, beyond any stage presentation, for the mind is as important as the body. Dancers have their own spirit, *kru*, but they also venerate their dance masters and the ancestors of dance, the supreme *kru*. These gurus of dance will guide, strengthen, protect and inspire them, bringing them success. The dancer is becoming, in Martha Graham's words, an athlete of god.

Classes continue until 11 am when the girls thank Soth Somaly with a *sampeah*, bowing and bringing joined hands to the lips, a sign of deep respect, and give thanks to the spirits. Then they scamper away, laughing, transformed from elegant *apsaras* back into jubilant children.

RUFA also has folk dancing and circus training. In these, students take classes with classical dancers at first and then learn folkloric dances that incorporate elements of the classical aesthetic and include masked dance, theatre and circus arts.

With luck, students might become part of the RUFA Classical Dance Troupe which has several leading performers and sometimes gives public performances and special events, or else they might enter the National Theatre Company of Cambodia. Otherwise, they might perform for tourists

The Apsara Arts Association, *Samakum Selapak*, funded by the Kasumisu Foundation with the help of American dance adviser Fred Frumberg, which started in 1998, trains orphans and children from underprivileged backgrounds in folk and classical dance. They run their school from a modest wooden house in Russei Keo, not far from the new RUFA campus.

Under the tutelage of Vong Metry, Sin Samadekchho and Chhay Sopha and choreographer Tith Sen, from the Royal University of Fine Arts, they learn folk dances such as as the Pailin Peacock Dance.

Dancer students practising.

Soth Somaly training a young dancer.

Below: **Underprivileged children and orphans learning to dance.**

Boys also study at RUFA.

CHAPTER 13 PREPARATION FOR PERFORMANCE

Preparing the bracelets for dance.

Below middle: **Male dancers ready to perform.**

Below right: **Applying heavy make-up.**

Apsara **dancer in costume.**

"Beneath the gorgeous costumes, the continuing significance of the dance is felt by the performers and communicated to the audience. It is in this aspect, especially, that the Eastern dance … can be seen as a true expression of a people's spiritual and social life,"
Gelsey Kirkland, *Dancing on My Grave.*

Costumes and makeup are an important and indispensable part of the stage performance. The gorgeous apparel enhances the fantasy aspect and ethereal nature of the roles enacted. Dancers wear opulent head-dresses, ornate jewellery and close-fitting silk costumes covered with sequins. Their feet remain bare. Before a performance, they are sewn into the costumes so that they are skin tight, and they must stand patiently for several hours while the glittering fabrics and spangles are stitched into place.

The princess, *neang*, wears a bodice *ao sbay*, of lace, covered with gold, a silk jacket, *ao pak*, a silk collar *srang kar*, a lamé *sampot*, and a brocade sash *sarabap*. *Sampots* for classical dance are created from gold and silver metallic thread supplementary weft-decorated cloth, s*ampot sarabap*. Women wear three pairs of arm bracelets, *kung dai*, *kravel day* and *partum*, anklets *kang choeng* and earrings, *tumhou*.

The prince, *neayrong*, is elegant and regal in a costume with epaulettes that give his appearance added strength. Masked demons wear a richly patterned *sampot chawng kbun*, over close fitting trousers, *kho snap*, of plain fabric, with a richly ornamented lower edge. Elaborately jewelled jackets, *ao pak*, are adorned with heavy gold chains across the chest, with a silk and brocade collar, *srang kar*. Men wear a brocade garment down to the knees, *choeung khor*. The belt is a *kravant*, which holds up the *sampot*. It is adorned with a jewelled stylet or stiletto in gold, *sang var*.

The women wear elaborate makeup which until recently consisted of a thick white paste made of lead and rice powder or alabaster powder. This made them appear more unreal, as if from the spirit world, as white is the colour of death in Asia, and it enhanced the magico-religious context. It used to be offset by blackened teeth and red stained lips, similar to the makeup of Japanese geishas. The contrast of the black and red against the pure white rendered the dancers more luminous in the darkened, candlelit performance area, heightening the drama. Today the cosmetics are more contemporary in style but still pronounced and theatrical.

Head-dresses and masks are the holiest part of the costume, just as the head is considered the holiest part of the body. Before being used they are placed on a table and offerings of flowers and incense are made to help their spirit to come alive. They are put on the head only when the dancer is fully dressed and made up. Head-dresses are sometimes topped with flowers, especially frangipani, the fragrant flower associated with the temple and prayers.

The female head-dress, or tiara, the *mkot*, of which there are five styles, is heavy to wear and used to be made of leather, cardboard, gold leaf and encrusted mirrors that sparkled with every movement. For the leading roles, it was made of gold. It can weigh as much as two kilos. Shaped like the spire of a shrine, it rises up in multiple tiers and, in emulation of the carved *apsaras* at Angkor, often features a diadem, which frames the forehead. Samdach Chaufea Thiounn[1] points out that the head-dress was the most expensive part of the costume, costing 800 piastres, and combined with the jewellery was worth 2,000 piastres.

Imbued with its own spirit, it is placed on the dancer's head only when the moment is right, with the dancer holding her hands in a gesture of prayer as this is done. It is the final stage of the costume preparation.

Male dancers wear masks for *lakhon kaol* and women wear them for *lakhon poul srei*, female masked drama. The wearing of masks for ceremonies and rituals has a long history associated not only with Hinduism but with many indigenous peoples. It is another of the Indian influences that found its way to Cambodia. Stylised masks with exaggerated expressions increase the emotional impact of the performance by portraying not only gods and demons but heroes and villains, as well as animals and birds. In the *Reamker*, the mask worn by Hanuman, Sva Sar, is white, Sugrib's is red and gold and those of the other monkeys, such as Nillaphat, Sva Khmao, is black, and Bali, the green monkey, is green. These cover the whole head, like a helmet. The mask worn by Krung Reab, king of the *yaks*, is also richly embellished with gold leaf.

Sam Sattya applying her make up.

Male dancers being stitched into their costumes.

One of the *yaks* outside Angkor Wat.

A teacher says prayers before placing a *mkot* on dancer's head.

A teacher places the *mkot* on a dancer's head as she holds her hands in gesture of prayer.

A dancer adjusts the heavy *mkot* on her head.

Head-dresses, *mkot*.

These ornate masks are made of clay and paper-mâché by a master mask maker who has trained in specialised techniques and knows all the characters. In the past, he would often have been a performing artist. One of the few master mask makers left today is An Sok, in his 60s, who works in Phnom Penh. He is trying to pass on his skills to a younger generation. It takes him about a month to make one mask.

To fabricate one, a mask maker will first sculpt the form in wet clay and then create a cement mould. He then attaches about ten strips of glue-soaked paper and cotton to the mould and paints them. After these have dried to form a mask, they are prized off the mould and left to harden. Elaborate decorative features are added afterwards. These are cast out of natural lacquer resin, found in a tree called the Kreul. The resin is heated and put into miniature moulds and when it has cooled the pieces are removed and fixed to the mask. Putting on the *mkot* and the masks is the final stage of the costume preparation.

The performers are now ready to re-enact the religious rituals of classical dance.

Rithy and Pich Kakada, the male wearing a Hanuman mask.

[1]*Danses cambodgiennes*, Samdach Chaufea Thiounn.

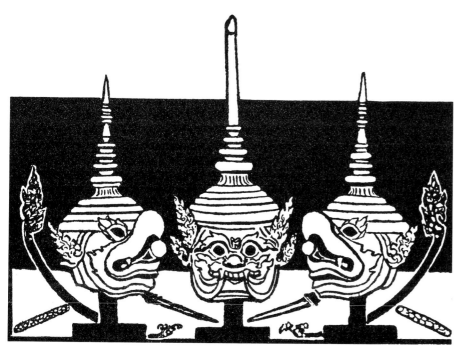

Master Seng Ly, a former dancer of *lakhon kaol*, one of the oldest living artists to have survived the killing fields. Between 1999-2002 he created 16 masks.

CHAPTER 14 PRESENT SITUATION AND FUTURE

Apsara on boarding pass.

Burned down Centre for
Performing Arts.

Burned down theatre.

"It is the mission of all art to express the highest and most beautiful ideals of man. What ideal does the ballet express? No, the dance was once the most noble of all arts; and it shall be again. From the great depth to which it has fallen, it shall be raised. The dancer of the future shall attain so great a height that all other arts shall be helped thereby." Isadora Duncan, Dancer, *The Dance of the Future.*

In recent years, there have been public performances by the National Theatre and the RUFA troupes all over the country and dance is now referred to as 'the soul of the nation,' helping to reinstate it as a treasured part of daily life of which Cambodians can be proud. On international tours, the graceful *apsaras* and musicians are viewed as the most precious resources of Cambodian culture. But in spite of progress and accolades, dancers still train and rehearse in adverse circumstances. While Angkor Wat, which appears on the country's flag, has been the international focus of cultural revival, support for dance is minimal. Although the royal government acknowledges that dance is important – one of the most ubiquitous images in Cambodia is that of the *apsara* dancers who appear on everything from tourist posters and adverts for hotels, restaurants and drinks to the boarding pass of one of the airlines – it has not, so far, set up an infrastructure for the intangible arts. A minute percentage of the national budget of the government is given to culture, leaving the burden to outside support and donations from other countries.

While Princess Buppha Devi was Minister of Culture between 1998 and 2003, progress was made through her efforts. The eldest of King Sihanouk's surviving children, with five children of her own, she felt a strong sense of responsibility for safeguarding Cambodia's artistic past. Members of the royal family have continued to learn to dance, including Princess Norodom Rattani Devi, daughter of Prince Norodom Ranariddh, Buppha Devi's brother, who became First Prime Minister in a coalition government with Hun Sen after the 1993 United Nations elections.

When Prince Norodom Sihamoni became king in

October 2004, a coronation that had crucial religious and symbolic overtones for Cambodians, with blessings by Buddhist monks, hopes were raised that the performing arts would become a priority because of his personal affiliations. When I interviewed him in 1995, he spoke of the tasks that lay ahead: "We have so much to do. Culture is so important. It is the soul of the people. If culture disappears, I am afraid for our people. I am afraid that culture will vanish. Everything is money, money, money. We need theatres, we need to train people, to train teachers. That is why I work with UNESCO." He said at the time that he wanted to consecrate his life to culture, to choreography and to film, and that he did not want to be king. However, circumstances changed and his political neutrality made him more suitable than other possible successors. Yet, even with his sense of commitment, much still remains to be done. Despite the talk of Siem Reap becoming a centre for the arts, this has not yet happened, even though it has been developed abundantly for tourism, the main strategy for socio-economic development and an important source of foreign income.

International donors have made generous contributions in the wake of the United Nations organised elections of 1993 which brought a more stable political situation. But performers, who are civil servants, are still impoverished. Until 2007 the National Theatre Company of Cambodia Classical Dance Troupe was still rehearsing in the burned out shell of the former Tonle Bassac Theatre which was destroyed by fire in 1994. Although it had never been restored it was still their official home. The derelict theatre, with its charred roof open to the skies, peeling walls and encroaching weeds, was originally built by renowned Cambodian architect Van Molyvann in the optimistic 1960s, and called the Preah Suramarit National Theatre. With its pyramidal roof and split level seating design for seating, it was inspired by the work of American architect Frank Lloyd Wright. The 1,200 seat theatre was given to the dancers by Prince Sihanouk in 1965. It was to here that they returned after the Pol Pot regime.

Em Theay with dancer Sok Chay on the morning
after the fire, February 1994.

Sophiline Cheam Shapiro rehearsing in
the burned down theatre.

Above and right: **Rehearsing in the burned down theatre.**

Above, right and below:
Rehearsals in the burnt out theatre.

Right: **The *pin peat* orchestra rehearse in the burnt out theatre.**

In February 1994, while renovation work was underway by a French company, a fire, believed to have been started by faulty wiring, tore through the theatre, which was not insured, almost burning it to the ground. The following morning, I went to report the story for the *Phnom Penh Post* and found Em Theay among the smoking ruins, bravely continuing lessons with her pupils outside under the palm trees, their only shade from the tropical heat. Nouth Narang, then the Minister of Culture, who had not signed any form of contract with the French company, launched an appeal for $12 million to rebuild the theatre, which succeeded only in offending the International Technological Committee responsible for the renovation and the French Embassy.

In response to the tragedy, Sihanouk offered the dancers temporary space in the Chanchaya Pavilion in the palace, but stated that he was unable to divert funds to the arts when people were still starving in the countryside. The French Embassy offered compensation, but this was channelled by the Council of Ministers to relief for those then affected by floods. Funds were apparently offered by Japan and China, some of which also went to flood relief, but what has happened in the intervening years is murky[1]. Nothing was done. The theatre's neglected state is almost a metaphor for the challenges facing contemporary dancers, and was used by Cambodian film director Rithy Pan for his elegiac film, *Les Artistes du theatre brulé*.

Now the site has now been leased to a private developer, and the building will have been razed by the time this book is published. According to Khim Sarith, secretary of state at the Ministry of Culture, it has been leased to a Cambodian tycoon, Kith Meng, who plans to develop a 'cultural building'. The 315 artists of the National Theatre Company have been offered $300 compensation each, and have been relocated to Mao Tse Tung Boulevard, to a smaller building that is not adequate for their needs, involving much further for each of them to travel on a daily basis.

Not only is there no proper theatre, but the Royal University of Fine Arts' performing arts campus was knocked down and the school and its classical dance ensemble forcibly banished to a distant and inhospitable suburb of Phnom Penh. Originally housed in an attractive collection of 1950s open-sided buildings in the northern part of the city, its land, having soared in value, was sold by the government in June 2005 and every edifice torn down. Fred Frumberg, head of the NGO Amrita Performing Arts, who had raised $20,000 for a theatre in the university grounds, was there on the last day and admitted that he wept when the bulldozers arrived. Students were performing final examinations, he recalled, and the bulldozers just kept going while teachers rushed into the offices to collect their files as the buildings collapsed. "It was eerie, bizarre," he said. Students and teachers now have to make their way to the hastily built school in Russei Keo, whose buildings are already cracking, nine kilometres northwest of Phnom Penh, a remote, barren area of landfill where they are sometimes mugged en route to classes. So difficult is the journey for the younger pupils, many have stopped coming to classes.

The dance companies are hampered by having no base to which audiences can gravitate. Without their own theatre, the National Theatre Company troupe of 248 artistes, among them dance and circus performers, earning just US$20 a month, cannot perform regularly.

For special occasions other buildings are used such as the Chaktamuk Conference Hall, also designed by Vann Molyvann, opened in 1961 and renovated in 2000, which seats nearly 600 people, and the Chenla Theatre, a municipal venue and cultural centre, originally a state cinema, used for conferences and film screenings. The National Cultural Centre, with its outdoor concrete stage, part of a national exhibition venue, sometimes doubles as a theatre, and ballrooms in hotels are occasionally used.

Siem Reap performances take place in hotels, restaurants and temple compounds and there are several dance schools there now, notably at the temple of Wat Raja Bo and the School of Arts. Performances are made possible by foreign donations or by NGOs, including Amrita Performing Arts and Krousar Thmey, a French-Cambodian project involved in helping children, especially orphans, become aware of their cultural heritage. Donations have come from numerous sources, including UNESCO, the Japan Foundation, the Toyota Foundation, New York's Asian Cultural Centre, the University of Bologna, the Rockefeller Foundation, the Danielle Mitterand Foundation, the American embassy and many others.

Attracting funding is one part of the future, but so also is the identity of dance and its practitioners as a new generation of performers emerge. Each time the companies go abroad, top dancers defect, including stars such as Yim Devi, escaping the uncertainty of conditions of home. In an art form which focuses on the beauty and youth of young women, dancers, who were once part of the royal harem, are inevitably offered opportunities to become mistresses or wives of important ministers and businessmen, thus enabling

The new RUFA campus.

Piseth Paeklica.

them to find financial security. They may then stop dancing. While in the bohemian circles of the West, especially in places such as Paris and New York, these liaisons could enhance the status of the dancer who becomes even more glamorous as a consequence, they can also result in tragedy. Piseth Paeklica, Cambodia's favourite classical dancer, was murdered in broad daylight at the height of her career, aged 34 years old, in 1999. She was rumoured to have been the mistress of the prime minister. There was a public outpouring of grief and 10,000 people attended her funeral. So the status and role of dancers is shifting with the changing circumstances of Cambodia itself.

Now that dance is no longer a ritual of the temple or a ceremony of the royal court, what is its future? Should contemporary dance, a popular form, evolve alongside the more esoteric traditional structures? Is it at risk of becoming a secular spectacle for tourists? Is it devalued by being divorced from its ritual context and placed in the commercial arena? Does this make it inauthentic? Should new creativity be brought to interpretations? Should productions reflect their era?

Like all classical ballet, the masterpieces are cherished. Their performance makes them a living archive. In the West, ballets such as Swan Lake constitute the canon of ballet and constantly play to packed theatres every season. Each new generation of balletomanes learns through watching such a performance. They preserve the formal values of harmony, clarity, order and symmetry where the academic technique is sacrosanct and the rules are never transgressed. Yet, while leading ballet companies in the West adhere faithfully to classics, there has also been an explosion of experimental dance forms in the 20th and 21st centuries pioneered by brilliant, innovative choreographers and dancers, ranging from Martha Graham to Glen Tetley, Pina Bausch to Twyla Tharp and Mikhail Baryshnikov to Sylvie Guillem. Guillem, for example, a ravishingly beautiful classical dancer who, with her extraordinary physique, has soared beyond the scope of any of her contemporaries, has worked with Akram Khan, an Indian dancer and choreographer. Uniting two exquisite theatrical forms from opposing disciplines, classical ballet and Indian *kathak*, Guillem worked with Khan's grounded *kathak* inheritance in a piece called *Sacred Monsters*, adopting a different vocabulary with slow, sculptural poses.

Contemporary dance is considered to be highly important by those helping in Cambodia such as Fred

Sylvie Guillem with Akram Kahn from Sadlers Wells. By kind permission of Mikki Kunttu.

Frumberg. "Classics can become like a museum," he points out. "They need to be living. But contemporary dance must never replace classical dance." He believes that the revival and preservation of classical dance has taken on its own momentum. "Classical dance is safe. It's here to stay." But, he writes[2], how does one keep the dance from from "becoming a precious gem hidden within a glass museum showcase?" Young artists have begun to ask these questions. For new inspiration Frumberg has, for example, praised Sophiline Cheam Shapiro and has brought choreographers from other parts of Asia to work with the dancers, such as the Javanese dancer and choreographer Miroto Martinus. From Malaysia, Australia and India came members of World Dance Alliance who conducted workshops. But groundbreaking aspects such as these have provoked conflict within the dance community, in particular elder masters, who are apprehensive about the task of reviving classical dance which is still not complete. Nevertheless Frumberg is adamant that Cambodia is ready to be included in the international contemporary dance community and young Cambodian dancers are seeking the tools with which they can create their own contemporary dance vocabulary. He believes that the emphasis must shift to creativity and productivity.

The king also spoke of the need for culture to develop when I interviewed him in 1995: "Dance has to move ahead in the world. Of course, we must keep the strict classical traditions intact, but another form, such as the folkloric dance, must open up, develop. It needs new form. It needs to be liberated. Western contemporary dance is more exubert, spontaneous. We talk about Angkor all the time. But too much emphasis is placed on Angkor. Glorious as it is, it's the past. It is the witness of a great culture, we must safeguard it. But now Cambodia needs other expressions."

The need for other expressions challenged dance traditions in countries such as Japan and Bali. In Japan, it resulted in the modern Butoh, Japan's experimental dance form which co-exists with traditional dance such as Bugaku and Kabuki. In Bali, visitors from the West have brought new changes to the classical canon and the creativity of the Balinese themselves has enriched and enlarged their repertory. The effect of tourism has been to strengthen rather than erode Balinese dance traditions. They are guaranteed an audience, in the form of visitors. Thus a fundamental pre-requisite has been achieved, since all performance requires participation in the form of spectators.

Like the Balinese, the Cambodians also preserve certain dances solely for their own sacred rituals. These are re-enacted by the same dancers who perform for tourists, showing how they are able to maintain the sacred dimension of dance while also marketing it for commercial purposes. In 2008, after I had watched dancers from RUFA perform on board a cruiseship, with the same reverence as in a temple, I asked them how they felt about it. They said they were proud to be showing their cultural traditions to foreigners who might otherwise never have seen them. The performance had meant as much to the dancers as any other that they might have given, as was indeed evident from the way they performed, and they were practical enough to know that this was the way to fund further artistic development.

The role of classical dance and the concern that, apart from tourist performances, it may be relegated to an elite status is questioned by directors such as Ong Keng Sen. In an interview[3], Ong Keng Sen, who has travelled extensively throughout Asia exploring the links as well as the paradoxes among Asian cultures, admitted: "The more consumerism takes over our city centres, the more the traditional arts have been relegated to the domain of universities and religious institutions. I don't think the average man in the street feels much of a connection with traditional culture."

But in spite of Ong Keng Sen's observation, dance has a strong image in Cambodia that extends throughout the country. As the temples of Angkor have become a tourist attraction, so also has dance. This is both advantageous and perilous. What was once the preserve of religious and royal ceremonies is now entertainment for the public. Poorly trained dancers perform in venues such as restaurants where the glamour of their costumes, glimpsed between courses of a meal, compensates for the tertiary standard of the entertainment, but is sufficient for spectators to imagine that they have absorbed authentic Cambodian culture. This kind of performance has become what scholars claimed that dance in the colonial period had become, namely, an art form that audiences think is part of the Angkorian tradition. But, since tourists will expect to see the classical dances, it is a way of perpetuating the tradition, making it more widely known and reinforcing its role in Cambodia today.

It is hoped that as Cambodian dance becomes better known throughout the world, choreographers, directors and dancers from other countries will come to exchange artistic ideas with Cambodia. Dance – and culture – does not exist in a vacuum. It is always changing, adapting, absorbing and developing. In order to survive physically, it must break into strands. If it becomes frozen, it loses its lifeblood. But, to survive spiritually, it must remain constant. Therefore, innovative ideas and new performers will contribute to the evolution of dance, but at its core the ritual re-enactment of ancient practices is the framework upon which everything else rests. Dance must exist in both theatres and temples. But in the former, it is still a religious ceremony.

In its purest form, perpetuated and taught in environments such as the Royal University of Fine Arts, dance will always be inextricably linked with sacred rituals. It is still regarded as a celebration of the gods. As such, it must be preserved, especially since the loss of a generation of dancers. Whereas the performance of a plays and music are drawn from scripts and scores, which can be interpreted in different ways, a dance production has no equivalent. It is ephemeral, existing only in performance. Even when filmed, it can never transmit the sublime qualities of the live performance.

Dance has restored a sense of beauty to a country that witnessed unimaginable horror. More than any other art form, it has rejuvenated national pride and encouraged a cultural rebirth.

[1]*Phnom Penh Post*, by Robert Turnbull, December 3-16, 2004.

[2]Fred Frumberg, *Dialogues in Dance Discourse: Creating Dance in Asia Pacific*, 2008.

[3]Ong Keng Sen, interviewed by journalist Robert Turnbull, 2007.

Scene from Pamina Devi, choreographed by Sophiline Cheam Shapiro.

CHAPTER 15 CONCLUSION

Single dancer, Angkor Wat.

Opposite: **Dancers at Angkor Wat, 1925.
Burton Holmes Historical Collection.**

Sunrise Angkor Wat.

"Respect the past, herald the future, but concentrate on the present." Dame Ninette de Valois, Royal Ballet, London.

If art is a reflection of a society, then the past must be preserved as inspiration for the present which in turn will shape the future. Dance has ebbed and flowed with Cambodia's turbulent history since the apogee of Angkor, almost disappearing and then re-emerging with a force that is inextinguishable. It seems to echo the cosmic dance of Shiva as he destroys and creates new worlds, in a continuous, cyclical process.

That dance returned in the aftermath of destruction with such strength is a testament to its redemptive and transcendent power. It shows not only the revival of a civilisation that vanished five hundred years ago, but the renewal of a society that was devastated 30 years ago. Dance has restored those myths that shape the spiritual framework for life, reminding Cambodian people of the gods, ancestors and heroes whose stories create a sense of harmony and completion. Giving aesthetic pleasure, dance transports the viewers who experience mimesis and catharsis as they are moved and purged by the representation. Order returns and the Hindu notions of the duality of existence with its eternal balance of opposites is re-established.

If Angkor Wat, a religious monument incorporating this perpetual balance, is the symbol of Cambodia, then the dancers who embody its cosmic rhythms are the soul. Dance is the quintessence of Cambodia.

When I first saw the dancers at Angkor Wat that day in 1993 it was like a resurrection. They had returned to the temple whose sacred rhythms they represented. The temple is a place of pilgrimage and to circumambulate it is to make a numinous journey that ends with redemption. As those tiny children danced, they were like symbols of hope after suffering, the cosmic after the chaotic. People like the old baker from the Grand Hotel who thought he would never see them again, had watched a rebirth, as his country completed a cycle and entered a new era.

Although this book is finished, it is not complete, because the story of Cambodian dance is evolving. In a rapidly changing country it will both influence and reflect the society which nurtures it. It has always been a celebration of the gods but today, more than ever, it is a celebration of the people of Cambodia.

GLOSSARY

Aaw nay Satin bodice worn by dancer

Amrita Elixir of immortality

Angkor Temple complex, former capital of the Khmer empire derived from the Sanskrit *nagara*, meaning holy city

Angkor Wat Most important temple at the site of Angkor

Ao pak Silk jacket

Ao sbay Lacebodice

Apsara Celestial dancer, celestial maiden

Arak Music invoking spirits

Asura Demon

Avatar Sanskrit for incarnation of deity

Bagavata Purana Early Indian texts

Bai Pka Tossing the flowers

Bangkok Capital of Siam (Thailand)

Banteay Srei Temple at Angkor

Banteay Samre Temple at Angkor

Bayon Temple at Angkor

Bhagavad Gita Song of the Lord, part of the *Mahabharata*

Boung Soung Ceremony to appeal to the *tevoda* to protect the kingdom

Boram apsara *Apsara* dance

Bourrées Rapid beating of the feet

Brahma One of the Hindu gods

Brahmin Member of the Hindu priestly caste

Buddha Enlightened One, founder of Buddhism, Prince Siddhart Gautama who lived in 6th century BC

Butoh Japanese experimental dance

Chakravartin Emperor of the world

Champa The empire of the Cham people who occupied southern Vietnam

Chapei Story telling

Chapei Dong Veng Two stringed, long necked guitar

Cheay kreng Side panels of costume

Chenla Early name of region of Cambodia

Chha banhchos Dance gestures

Chha banhchos Vocabulary of dance gestures and poses

Chhing Cymbals

Choeung khor Brocade male dancer's trousers down to the knees

Chrieng Chapei Chanted story

Chrieng tar Improvised ballads

Comédies-ballets Mixtures of plays with dance interludes

Corps de ballet Ballet company

Demi-plié The fourth position in Western classical ballet

Deva God

Devaraja God-king of the Khmer empire

Devata Female Khmer divinity

École des Beaux Arts School of Fine Arts

École Francaise d'Extrème Orient French School of the Far East

Entam Shoulder ornaments

Funan Early name of region of Cambodia

Garuda The mythical half bird, half man, which carried Vishnu on his back

Gopura Gateway to temple

Guru Spiritual Guide

Guru-shishya parampara The Indian tradition of teachers and disciples

Hanuman Monkey hero of the *Ramayana*

Haut relief High relief, three dimensional carving

Hevajra Dancing deity in Bayon style

Hinduism Polytheistic religion of India, one of the oldest in the world, and of the Khmer empire

Homrong Musician's prayer

Hora Palace astrologers

Indochina French name for the Union of Cambodia, Laos and Vietnam

Indra Hindu god of war

Jatakas Stories of the Buddha's lives

Kang choeng Ankle rings

Kangkan, kangrak Arm bracelets

Kbach Movements of dance, cadence

Khmer Language of Cambodia and of the Khmer Empire

Khmer Rouge Cambodian guerrilla soldiers of Pol Pot

Kho snap Men's loose-fitting trousers

Khom thom Semi-circular arrangement of gongs

Khon Siamese male masked drama

Khse khluon Chains on chest of costume

Krama Traditional Cambodian scarf

Kravant Belt

Kravel choeng Filigree anklets

Kré Low table at dance performances

Krishna An incarnation of the god Vishnu

Kru Cambodian word for guru

Lakhon Dance drama

Lakhon ayai Improvised folk chant

Lakhon bassac Popular performing arts

Lakhon fai nai Siamese female dance drama

Lakhon kbach boran Ancient drama, often called *lakhon luong* (or *lueng*)

Lakhon luong King's dancers

Lakhon mohori Folkloric and musical forms

Lakhon poul srei Female masked drama

Lakhon preah reach troap Dance repertoire of the Court

Lakhon sbaek thom Shadow theatre

Lakhon yike Folkloric and musical forms

Lakshmana Brother of Rama in the *Reamker*

Langka The Kingdom in the *Reamker*

Lingam Phallic symbol of Shiva

Mahabharata Ancient Hindu epic from India

Mandala a generative symbol in architectural form

Mekhala Belt

Mekong River running through Cambodia

Mission civilisatrice France's civilising mission

Mkot Coronet of dancer

Mount Meru Home of the gods, a mountain at the centre of the universe

Mudra Sacred gesture or pose of the Buddha

Naga A multi-headed snake, guardian deity

Nagara Holy city

Nagi Dragon princess

Nataraja Shiva as Lord of the Dance

Natya Sastra of Bharata Ancient Sanskrit treaty on dramaturgy

Nang sbaek Shadow puppets

Neak ta Supernatural forces

Neang Princess

Neayrong Prince

Nelumbium speciosum The pink lotus

Nirvana Literally nothingness, release from earthly ties

Nymphaea The white Lotus of ancient Egypt

Nymphaea caerulea The blue lotus sacred to Vishnu

Pali Ancient Indic language in which the Buddhist canon is written

Phleng kar Marriage song

Phleng mohori Kind of chanting

Phleng pin peat Traditional orchestra of Cambodia

Phnom Penh Capital of Cambodia

Piphat Siamese musical ensemble

Plié Bended knees movement in classical ballet

Preah Ream Cambodian version of Rama, hero of the *Ramayana*

Premieres danseuses Leading dancers

Raja King

Robam Dance

Robaing muk Panel of cloth on costume

Roneat Percussion instrument

Rakshasas Demons

Ramayana Ancient Hindu Epic

Rasa Hindu aesthetic theory

Ravana Wicked demon of the *Ramayana*

Reamker Cambodian version of the *Ramayana*

Rig Veda Ancient Sanskrit hymns

Robam boran Ancient classical dance

Robam Chuon Po Flower blessing dance

Roeung Dance dramas

Samhara Destruction

Sampeah The bow with hands joined in prayer made in greeting

Sampeah Kru Prayer to guru

Sampho Drum

Sampot Wraparound skirt traditional in Cambodia

Sampot chawng kbun Part sarong, part trousers

Sampot sarabap Silver metallic thread supplementary weft-decorated cloth

Sangkum Reastr Niyum People's Socialist Community

Sang var Stiletto in gold

Sanskrit Early Indic language

Sarabap Brocade sash

Sbaek thom Large shadow puppet

Sbaek touch Small shadow puppets

Sbay Velvet scarf

Seda Cambodian version of Sita, heroine of the *Ramayana*

Shiva Hindu god of creation and destruction

Shrishti Creation

Siam early name of Thailand, changed in 1930s under Prime Minister Phibun

Siem Reap Town at Angkor

Skoor thom A double-sided drum

Sleek por Pendant

Son et lumière Sound and light show

Songkhran New year water festival

Srang kar Silk collar

Srely Oboe

Sri Lanka Former Ceylon

Sthiti Preservation

Sukhothai Thai kingdom

Sumad-atmajas Heavenly daughters of pleasure

Suranganas Wives of the gods

Sur la pointe On pointed toe

Sutras Sermons of the Buddha

Sva Monkey

Tantra Buddhist philosophy

Tevoda Celestial being

Theatre celeste Celestial theatre

Theravada Buddhism Doctrine of the Elders, the branch of Buddhism that spread across southeast Asia

Tirobhava Illusion

Tonle Sap Lake in the centre of Cambodia

Topeng Javanese mask dance

Tribhanga Pose with hips slanted and weight on one leg

Trimurti Trinity of gods, constituting destroyer, creator and preserver

Tumhou Earrings

Vaastu shastra The science of Indian architecture founded on divine geometry

Vishnu Hindu god of preservation and compassion

Wat Buddhist or Hindu Temple

Wayang kulit Javanese shadow play

Yaks Demons or giants

SELECTED BIBLIOGRAPHY

Banha, Martin (Ed.), *The Cambridge Guide to World Theatre*, 1988

Bouillevaux, Charles Emile, *Voyages dans l'Indochine 1848-1856*, 1858

Burckhardt, Titus, *Sacred Art in East and West*, Perennial Books, 1967

Busy, Leon, *A l'Ombre d'Angkor: Cambodge dans les années vingt*, Albert Kahn, 1992

Cass, Joan, *Dancing through History*, Prentice Hall publishers, 1993

Catlin, Amy, *Apsara: The Feminine in Cambodian Art*, Apsara Media for Intercultural Education, 1987

Cambodia Arts Directory, Visiting Arts, 2001

Chandler, David P, *History of Cambodia*, Silkworm Books, 1994

Chandler, David P, *Brother Number One – A Political Biography of Pol Pot*, Silkworm Books, 1999

Chou Ta-Kuan, *Customs of the People of Cambodia*, 1296

Clarke, Joyce Ed., *Bayon – New Perspectives*, River Books, 2007

Coleridge, Samuel Taylor, *Biographia Literaria*, 1817

Coomaraswamy, Ananda K., *The Dance of Shiva, The Dance of Shiva: Fourteen Indian Essays*, Noonday Press, 1957

Cooper, Nichola, *France in Indochina, Colonial Encounters*, Berg, 2001

Cravath, Paul, *Earth in Flower: An Historical and Descriptive Study of Classical Dance Drama of Cambodia*, University of Hawaii, 1985

Cravath, Paul, *Earth in Flower: The Divine Mystery of Cambodian Dance Drama*, DatAsia Inc, 2008

Crisp, Clement and Clarke, Mary, *The History of Dance*, Orbis Publishing, 1981

Dagens, Bruno, *Angkor Heart of an Asian Empire*, Thames and Hudson/New Horizons, 1989, translated 1995

Delaporte, Louis, *Voyage au Cambodge: L'architecture Khmer*, Paris (Delagrave) 1880

Edwards, Penny, '*Womanising Indochina: Colonial Cambodia*' in *Domesticating the Empire* by Julia Clancy-Smith and Frances Gouda, University of Virginia Press 2007

Ghosh, Amitav, *Dancing in Cambodia*, Granta, 1998

Groslier, Bernard-Philippe, *Indochina*, Methuen, 1962

Groslier, George, *Danseuses cambodgiennes anciennes et modernes*, 1913

Grunfeld, Frederick V. *Rodin, A Biography*, 1987

Harrison, Tony, *Prometheus*, Faber & Faber, 1998

Havelock Ellis, Henry, *The Dance of Life*, Houghton Mifflin Company, 1923

Hideo, Sasagawa, *Post Colonial Discourses on the Cambodian Court Dance*, Institute of Asian Studies, Sophia University, Japan, Southeast Asian Studies Vol 42, No 4, March 2005

Higham, Charles, *The Civilization of Angkor*, Weidenfeld & Nicolson, 2001

Hodgson, Terry, *The Batsford Dictionary of Drama*, BT Batsford, 1988

Ingleton, Sally, *The Tenth Dancer*, Film, Singing Nomads/IBT Production for BBC TV, 1992

Isadora Duncan, *Dancer, 1878-1827, The Dance of the Future*, Theatre Arts Book, New York, Copyright 1928 by Helen Hackett, Inc, renewed copyright 1969 by Theatre Arts Books

Jacob, Judith M (with assistance of Haksrea, Kuoch), *Reamker, Cambodian Version of the Ramayana*, Royal Asiatic Society, 1986

Jacques, Claude, *Angkor, Cities and Temples*, River Books, 1997

Jeldres, Julio, *The Royal House of Cambodia*, Monument Books, 2003

Jonas, Gerald, *Dancing*, BBC Books, 1992

Keay, John, *Mad About the Mekong*, Harper Collins 2005

Kirkland, Gelsey, *Dancing on My Grave*: Hamish Hamilton, 1986

Krasosvskaya, Vera, *Nijinsky*, Schirmer Books, 1974

Kravel, Pich Tum, *Sbek Thom: Khmer Shadow Theater*, Southeast Asia Program, Cornell University, UNESCO, 1995

Laurent, Monique, *Rodin*, Grange Books, 1994

Lobban, William, '*Making the Traditional Musical Instruments of Cambodia*', *Cultural Survival Quarterly*, Issue 14.3, July 31, 1990

Loti, Pierre, *Un Pelerin d'Angkor*, 1912

Loviny, Christophe, *Les danseuses Sacree d'Angkor*, published by Seuil/Jazz editions

MacDonald, Malcolm, *Angkor*, Jonathan Cape, 1958

Malaysian Ministry of Culture, Arts and Heritage, *Dialogues in Dance Discourse: Creating Dance in Asia Pacific*, 2007

Malraux, André, *The Royal Way*, 1935

Marchal, Sappho, *Khmer Costumes and Ornaments of the Devatas of Angkor Wat*, 1927, republished Orchid Press, 2005

Mehta, Julie, *Dance Of Life*: *The Mythology, History, and Politics of Cambodian Culture*, Graham Brash Pte Ltd, 2001

Musée Rodin, *Rodin and the Cambodian Dancer His Final Passion*, 2006

Phim, Toni Samantha, *Cambodian Dance*, Oxford University Press, 1999

Phim, Toni Shapiro, *Tradition and Innovation in Cambodian Dance*, Philadelphia Folklore Project Southeast Asia Outreach Programme Office

Pou, Saveros, *Selected Papers on Khmerology 1967-2002*, Reyum Publishing, 2003

Prior, Marge, *Shooting At the Moon*, MPA Publishing 1994

Rawson, Philip, *The Art of Southeast Asia*, Thames & Hudson, 1967

Rawson, Philip, *The Art of Tantra*, Thames & Hudson, 1973

Roveda, Vittorio, *Khmer Mythology*, River Book 1997

Said, Edward, *Orientalism*, 1978

Said, Edward, *Culture and Imperialism*, 1993

Shawn, Ted, *Gods Who Dance*, E P Dutton & Co 1925

Short, Philip, *Pol Pot: The History of a Nightmare*, John Murray, 2004

Thiounn, Samdach Chaufea, *Danses Cambodgiennes*, drawings by Sappho Marchal, Institut Bouddhique, 1927

Thomson, John, *Antiquities of Cambodia*, 1867

Tully, John, *France on the Mekong*, University Press of America, 2002

Waterstone, Richard, *India: The Cultural Companion*, Duncan Baird Publishers, 1995

Zarina, Xenia, *Royal Cambodian Dances, Classic Dances of the Orient*, Crown Publishers, 1967

Fonds Iconographique des Missions Étrangères, www.archivesmep.mepasie.org

Krousar Thmey, www.krousar.thmey.org

Cambodian Living Arts, website: http://www.cambodianlivingarts.org
UNESCO's website: http://www.unesco.org

Apsara Arts Association, France: tel +01 72 81 30 39 tel +855-11-857-424, http://www.apsara-art.org

Cambodia Trust, www.cambodiatrust.org.uk

ACKNOWLEDGEMENTS

I am deeply indebted to Princess Norodom Buppha Devi for the help and time she gave me.

I am especially grateful to Narisa Chakrabongse and Paisarn Piammattawat for their enthusiasm, support and recommendations for this book. I am also very grateful to the late Philip Jones Griffiths for the gift of his photograph.

Thanks also to the numerous people who helped me with ideas, guidance and constructive criticism, including Christopher Benstead, Alain Daniel, Damian Heywood, Dr Angela Hobart, H E Hor Nambora, Ambassador of Cambodia to the United Kingdom, Dr Vittorio Roveda, Robert Turnbull, Kousoum Saroeuth, Director General of Tourism, Cambodia, Plong Thoeun, Ministry of Tourism, the Phnom Penh Hotel, the Juliana Hotel, Phnom Penh, the staff of the Royal Academy of Dance Library.

INDEX

Numbers in bold denote illustrations. Khmer names are indexed by first name, non-Khmer names by surname.

10/09